PATTERN CUTTING PRIMER

First published in Great Britain in 2012
Bloomsbury Publishers
50 Bedford Square, London WC1B 3DP
www.acblack.com

ISBN 978-1-4081-5667-4

Printed in China

Art Director: Emily Portnoi
Design concept: Emily Portnoi
Artwork and layout: Rebecca Stephenson
Commissioning Editor: Isheeta Mustafi
Illustrations: Jo Barnfield

PATTERN CUTTING PRIMER

ALL YOU NEED TO KNOW ABOUT DESIGNING, ADAPTING & CUSTOMISING SEWING PATTERNS

JO BARNFIELD & ANDREW RICHARDS

BLOOMSBURY

CONTENTS

INTRODUCTION: PATTERN ANNOTATIONS   6

① THE BASICS   8

CHAPTER 1: TOOLS, SUPPLIES AND EQUIPMENT   10

CHAPTER 2: FUNDAMENTALS OF A GARMENT   16
- Seams   16
- Darts   26

CHAPTER 3: FABRIC CONSIDERATIONS   30
- Interfacings   30
- Other forms of support   32
- Layout, cutting and marking   34
- Order of make   42

② DRAFTING TECHNIQUES   46

CHAPTER 4: DESIGNING PATTERNS FROM SCRATCH   48
- Taking measurements   48
- Making basic blocks   50
- Pattern design essentials   56
- Dart manipulation   60
- Combining and dividing   68
- Creating your own pattern blocks   72
- Toiles   77

CHAPTER 5: FITTING PRINCIPLES AND PATTERN ADJUSTMENTS   78

CHAPTER 6: RUB-OFF PATTERN DRAFTING   94

3

PATTERN DEVELOPMENT 104

CHAPTER 7: VOLUME AND SUPPRESSION 106
- Volume 106
- Gathering 112
- Pleats 114

CHAPTER 8: SLEEVES 116

CHAPTER 9: COLLARS 124

CHAPTER 10: WAISTBANDS AND CUFFS 130
- Waistbands 130
- Cuffs 134

CHAPTER 11: OPENINGS AND FASTENINGS 136
- Openings 136
- Fastenings 146

CHAPTER 12: FINISHINGS, LININGS AND FACINGS 152
- Hemming 152
- Facings 154
- Linings 158

CHAPTER 13: POCKETS 164

4

THE DESIGNER MAKER 174

CHAPTER 14: GOING PRO 176
- Design development 178
- Technical considerations 182
- Promoting your work 184

GLOSSARY 186
RESOURCES 189
INDEX 190
ACKNOWLEDGEMENTS 192

INTRODUCTION

PATTERN ANNOTATIONS

Proper pattern annotation is the main form of communication on the pattern piece; it is vital that it is clear and informative. For the sewing machinist it ensures that the garment can be properly constructed, that each piece of a pattern is present and that seam allowances, notches and dart positions are in place and are accurate.

MARKING LINES

Some of the main information on the pattern indicates the following:

- The cut line and stitch line. These denote the edges of the allowance needed to seam the garment. Tracing the pattern off to the stitch line gives a nett pattern, which is best used if the pattern needs to be altered.
- Grainline. The grainline has arrows at either end to show direction. (NB: a red, arrowed line is used in this book to indicate the grainline.)
- Centre front (CF) and centre back (CB).
- The main horizontal body measurement lines, such as waist, hip, bust (including the bust point).
- 'Place on fold' bracket, indicating that the pattern piece should be placed on to folded fabric to create a mirrored piece once cut.
- Cut right side up (Cut RSU) or occasionally cut wrong side up (Cut WSU). Right side and wrong side may be abbreviated as RS and WS respectively.
- Left-hand side (LHS) and right-hand side (RHS).
- Darts and pocket positions indicated by a punched drill hole in the pattern.
- Pleat direction marked with an arrow from fold to end position.
- Interior cut lines such as for a placket opening on a sleeve.
- Fold lines such as on a button stand or pleat.
- Roll lines such as the soft roll line of a collar or break line of a rever.
- Hemline.
- Fastening positions for buttons and buttonholes, zips and so on.

ANNOTATION SHOULD INCLUDE:

- The garment name or style code, e.g., Raglan Sleeve Raincoat.
- The garment grade, e.g., size 12.
- The pattern piece, e.g., sleeve, pocket flap.
- The number of the piece, e.g., piece 2 of 8.
- An explanation for the cutter, e.g., cut 1 pair self and fusing, cut on fold, etc.
- Seam allowance, e.g., 1cm (⅜in) SA, Nett, etc.
- The date, or the version number.

If you are working in a team, it is also helpful to include the name or initials of the pattern designer who created the pattern.

COMMON PATTERN ANNOTATION

NAME	DESCRIPTION	ANNOTATION
Pattern adjustment lines	Two parallel lines indicate lengthening or shortening position.	
Grainline	Indicates the direction the pattern piece should be laid on to fabric. A coloured line has been used throughout this book to indicate grain direction.	
Cut on fold	Denotes pattern piece that should be cut on a folded piece of fabric.	
Cut line (single size)	Indicates the cut line.	
Cut line (multi-size)	A commercial dressmaking pattern contains multiple sizes on one tissue; in industry this is called a graded nest. This line may be solid or dashed.	
Stitch line	Not all commercial patterns indicate the stitch line, especially ones that contain multiple sizes.	
Notches	Triangle-shaped marks that indicate positions on individual seams that need to be lined up during construction. A double triangle indicates a back pattern piece.	
Pleat symbols	Indicate pleat position and pleat fold direction.	
Button position	Marks the placement of buttons.	
Buttonhole position	Marks the placement of buttonholes.	
Drill hole	Can indicate precise matching or construction points.	

1

THE BASICS

CHAPTER 1: TOOLS, SUPPLIES AND EQUIPMENT   10

CHAPTER 2: FUNDAMENTALS OF A GARMENT   16
- Seams   16
- Darts   26

CHAPTER 3: FABRIC CONSIDERATIONS   30
- Interfacings   30
- Other forms of support   32
- Layout, cutting and marking   34
- Order of make   42

CHAPTER 1:
TOOLS, SUPPLIES AND EQUIPMENT

It is important to understand the tools of the pattern-cutting trade before you start. Some are essential (such as a measuring tape) or multifunctional (such as Patternmaster) and you will use them constantly; others have a specific use (e.g., a pattern notcher) and you will need them less often. These tools can be accumulated over time, and you may form your own equipment preferences as you work.

PATTERN-CUTTING EQUIPMENT

ESSENTIAL ITEMS
These items are essential if you want to create professional patterns.

- **Tape measure:** Used for taking body measurements and measuring curves on pattern pieces. (1)

- **Metal ruler:** A metre- or yard-length metal ruler keeps a true straight line. A smaller 30cm (12in) metal ruler is also useful. (2)

- **Set square:** This ensures that lines run true at 90 degrees on a pattern. (3)

- **French curves:** Use for forming smaller curves such as collars. (4)

- **Awl:** This tool can be used to make small holes in pattern pieces. It can also be used to help pivot darts accurately. (5)

- **Tracing wheel:** This is used to trace through both paper and fabric to mark lines and positions with a continuous line of small pinpricks on a piece of paper underneath. (6)

- **Pattern paper and card:** These are also essential for creating pattern drafts and 'working' (in process) patterns. Pattern paper is very thin and can be traced through, while pattern card is more hardwearing (not shown).

ALSO USEFUL
The following items may be useful in pattern-cutting, but are not so fundamental.

- Pattern notcher (7)
- Patternmaster (8)
- Hip curve (9)
- Flexible curve (10)
- T-square (11)
- Pattern drill (12)
- Shoben marking tape or style tape (13)
- Mannequin (not shown)

THE BASICS

Tools, supplies and equipment

GARMENT CONSTRUCTION EQUIPMENT

ESSENTIAL ITEMS

The following are essential in the process of garment construction.

- **Shears:** Large scissors with blades over 15cm (6in) long. (1)

- **Embroidery scissors:** Small precision scissors for cutting to exact points and trimming threads. (2)

- **Pins:** These hold garment sections in position for seaming, and pattern to paper when cutting out. (3)

- **Unpicker:** Used to quickly undo an incorrect seam. (4)

- **Tweezers:** A precision tool whose many purposes include threading machinery. (5)

- **Hand-sewing needles:** These include crewels (embroidery needles), sharps (short hand-sewing needles), betweens and blunts (shorter needles used by tailors on heavy fabrics). (6)

- **Lint brush:** This will help to raise pile on fabrics, as well as removing fluff (not shown).

ALSO USEFUL

- Rotary cutter (7)
- Fabric weights (8)
- Fabric sealant (not shown)

MARKING TOOLS

ESSENTIAL ITEMS

Note that all marks on fabric should be temporary; test these methods before use on fabric to find the most suitable.

- **Tailor's chalk:** This is available in many colours, and is one of the most traditional methods used to create temporary marks on the fabric. These chalks can blunt quickly; however, there are tools available that use chalk dust to produce continuous, fine, sharp chalk lines. (1)

- **Cloth-marking pencils and pens:** A chalk pencil can be quite waxy and not easily removed from fabric. Cloth-marking pens use ink that either disappears within 24 hours or can be removed with water. They are commonly double-ended with an ink-removal solution at the other end if you want to erase markings immediately. (2)

- **Thread tracing:** This is another way of marking fabric: a type of running stitch that is visible as a line on both sides of the fabric (not shown).

ALSO USEFUL
- Chalk sharpener (3)

PRESSING TOOLS

Pressing is fundamental to a well-made garment.

- **Press cloth:** A press cloth is a piece of fabric, usually cotton, that you can put over fabric when pressing so the iron does not damage the fabric (not shown).

- **Ham:** Derived from the traditional word for buttocks, the tailor's ham is used to press three-dimensional shapes; for example, in bust or hip shaping. (1)

- **Sleeve board:** This is a narrow padded board for pressing sleeves and sleeveheads, as well as other tubular garment shapes that cannot be pressed flat on the ironing board. (2)

- **Iron cleaner:** A metal cleaner used for cleaning the metal base of an iron (not shown).

USING A SEWING MACHINE

Domestic sewing machines usually serve a variety of purposes, whereas machines used in industry are often specific to one purpose (for example, an overlocker).

ESSENTIAL FEATURES

The following are the essential considerations when using a domestic sewing machine for putting together your designs.

- **Sewing machine:** This is an all-purpose machine, with various stitches for seams, decorative embroidery stitches and buttonholes. Designed for the home user, it is unsuitable for heavy industrial use. (1)

- **Machine needles:** The type and weight of fabric dictates which needle you should use. A standard needle has a pointed tip and is suitable for most wovens; leather needles have a tip more similar to a blade, to cut into the material rather than to pierce it; jersey/knit needles have a ballpoint, or rounded head, so as not to damage or snag the knit. Each of these needles is available in many sizes, with finer needles more suitable for lightweight fabrics, and thicker needles for heavier ones. (2)

- **Machine threads:** Threads are available in many weights and fibre compositions. The type of thread used is determined both by the weight of the fabric and its purpose, whether for seaming or topstitching. (3)

- **Bulk threads:** Bulk threads are a loosely twisted polyester thread; used for an overlocker, this type of thread gives a flat appearance (not shown).

MACHINE FEET

Depending on the make and model of your machine, a range of feet is available:

- **Plain foot:** For most general machine-stitching. (4)

- **Teflon foot:** A Teflon-coated plastic foot for use on slippery fabrics and some leathers. (5)

- **Velvet foot:** A narrow foot for fabrics with a heavy pile such as velvet and velour. (6)

- **Zipper feet:** These are available in left- and right-side versions. (7)

- **Invisible/concealed zipper foot:** A small foot with grooved guides for attaching invisible or concealed zips. (8)

ALSO USEFUL

- A narrow foot is able to stitch closely to an edge. Used mostly for attaching plain zips, but also for piping (not shown).

- Binding attachments are handy for producing bound seams and hems in one step (not shown).

- Gathering feet are useful for creating an even gather (not shown).

make and size
shank
long groove
shaft
short groove/scarf
eye
point

CHAPTER 2: FUNDAMENTALS OF A GARMENT

SEAMS

Seams are lines of stitching that join together individual garment sections. The type of seam used is determined by elements such as fabric (its thickness, whether it has stretch and so on); the desired look (a certain seam may help to impart a certain feel, such as a machine-felled seam for workwear or jeans); and the location of the seam (whether a stronger, more durable seam is most appropriate).

PREPARING TO SEW SEAMS

Check the machine tension on a scrap of the fabric before you sew. The stitch should be flat and regular, not puckered or loopy. Sewing problems can stem from incorrect tension, machine threading, stitch length, needle size or a blunt or bent needle.

A seam guide can be used to keep a constant, accurate seam width. However, with experience you will become less reliant on it and be able to visualise a precise seam allowance in relation to the foot width.

With certain exceptions, each seam must be backstitched by sewing back and forth for a couple of stitches at the start and finish of the seam. This secures the seam and prevents it from opening up.

An alternative to backstitching is to tie off the threads at both ends. This is more of a couture finish, but there are times when this is appropriate for certain fabrics.

At the end of each seam, threads must be trimmed, and the seam pressed in preparation for the next stage. A seam should be almost invisible when sewn; however, decorative seaming and topstitching can be used to enhance style lines within a garment.

MATCHING THE THREAD

Use the correct thread for the fabric that you are using, matching it as closely as possible to the fabric colour. If a perfect match cannot be found, go for a slightly lighter tone, as the thread will tend to look darker when the seam is constructed. You should also consider matching thread for appropriate weight and fibre content.

MATCHING SEAMS

Seams must be matched accurately; there are ways to ensure this,
as explained below.

PINNING

Pins are available in many types and thicknesses. It is important to choose
an appropriate pin size for the fabric used, so it does not leave pinholes that
cannot be removed. Certain materials, such as leather, PVC or waxed or
coated fabrics cannot be pinned for this reason; paperclips can be used
instead, or take care to pin just within the seam allowance, so that any pin
marks will not show.

stitch line

WS

When pinning, secure pieces together at each end first, then at notches
and centre, and lastly between these points at 7.5–10cm (3–4in) intervals.
Too many pins can hinder construction. Take care to remove pins while
you are sewing; sewing over a pin can result in either a broken needle
or an irregular stitch line.

It is best to pin across, rather than down, the seam, as this helps to secure
points together more accurately. When trying to match two seams that cross
through one another, match seams at the stitch line and pin 1.2cm (½in) on
either side. Pinning here rather than on the seam means that the seams are
less likely to slip on one another, and are more likely to line up precisely.

TACKING

Tacking is a form of running stitch, hand-sewn along the stitch line.
It is used to keep sections together temporarily for machine sewing.
The tacking stitch is a large stitch usually made in a contrasting colour
thread. It is unsecured at either end so that it can be removed easily.

Tacking can be more suitable than pins for insetting sleeves, as it gives
an opportunity to check correct balance on the wearer before it is finally
sewn by machine. It can help to more accurately allocate tolerance (ease)
within a seam, such as on a sleevehead.

Tacking can also be used to stabilise two layers of fabric that form one
garment section. Here, the stitch is sewn around the edge of the pattern
pieces on the seam allowance.

STAYSTITCHING

Staystitching is a permanent line of stitches made 1.2cm (½in) from the cut edge of a garment section. It helps prevent the piece from stretching and distorting, especially in curved areas such as the neckline or armhole.

lay tape over stitch line and sew to garment section before joining the seam

TAPING SEAMS

A cotton tape sewn onto the seam allowances can be used to support a seam, such as on the shoulder, and stop it from stretching. (1)

DIRECTIONAL SEWING

The direction in which you sew garment sections together plays a key part in construction. Sewing against the grain on a bias or curve can stretch the seam. It is usually best to sew the straightest part of a seam first, such as from hem to waistline on a skirt. Shoulder seams should be constructed from neck to shoulder; side bodice seams from underarm to waist. The exception is fabrics with a pile or nap, which must be sewn upwards with the direction of the pile.

TRIMMING SEAMS

Seams can be trimmed back to 4mm (³⁄₁₆in), or graded by trimming back seam allowances to different widths, say 4 and 7mm (³⁄₁₆ and ⁵⁄₁₆in). This removes bulk from the seam allowance and allows seams to lay flatter. Grading ensures that seam allowances do not leave a visible ridge from the right side.

FINISHING SEAMS

If a garment is not lined, seam edges must be finished to prevent them fraying. Some types of seam, such as welt and French seams, are self-neatening – they are finished in the process of construction. However, most need to be neatened through overlocking or binding. Seam finishing should be done as the garment is being made, and before one section is sewn to another.

TYPES OF SEAMS

There are many ways in which two garment parts can be joined, depending on the style and nature of the garment, the fabric type and the location of the seam. The following are principal seaming techniques.

PLAIN SEAM

A plain seam is the most commonly used method of garment construction. To sew a plain seam:

plain seam, WS

Right sides of fabric are placed together and a single line of stitch is made on the stitching line (usually 1–1.5cm/⅜–⅝in).

plain seam, open, WS

The seam allowances can be splayed and pressed to give an open seam, which gives the flattest finish from the right side.

plain seam, closed, WS

The seam allowances can be pressed to one side, giving a closed seam, to create a slightly raised look to one edge.

plain seam, RS

The completed seam from the right side.

EDGE-STITCHED SEAM

Edge-stitching is a line of topstitching made close to the edge of a seam. It is both decorative and functional, strengthening the seam and keeping areas such as facings in place. Edge-stitching, like topstitching, is usually made in a longer stitch length than that of the seam.

edge-stitched seam, open, WS

edge-stitched seam, closed, WS

THE BASICS
Fundamentals of a garment

UNDER-STITCHING

Under-stitching is a single row of edge-stitch. It is used to stop profile edges, such as the neckline, armhole, waistband facing or lining, from rolling outwards. This stitch line is not seen on the outer shell.

When the seam attaching the garment inner is sewn, lightly press both seam allowances inwards towards the facing/lining, then sew the under-stitch row from the right side of the garment. This catches the seam allowances underneath.

Finished under-stitching from right side.

SEWING A CORNER SEAM

A corner seam is comprised of a corner piece and an 'insert' section. You can press the seam allowances at the corner of both sections, or use a marking pen to act as an 'invisible' crease guide to follow when sewing; this helps to indicate the exact pivot point of the corner. To sew a corner seam:

Place the corner piece right side up on the machine, then place the insert section right side down on top of this, matching the stitch lines of one side of the corner (you can't match both edges due to the angle). Stitch from the edge of the seam to the point of the corner. When you reach this point, keep the needle down in the fabric. Dropping down to a smaller stitch length from around 2.5cm (1in) from the corner point can give more accuracy.

With the needle still down, raise the machine foot and snip into the corner section, to within two threads of the needle. Now the corner section will be released and you will be able to turn this section (pivoting on the needle) to meet the other side of the corner insert, to complete the seam.

The finished seam as seen from the wrong side.

INCOMPLETE UNDER-STITCHING

The shape of garment sections – a rever collar or shaped facing, for instance – may dictate that under-stitching cannot be completed around the whole of a seam.

MITREING CORNERS

Mitreing corners cuts away bulk, which if left would stop the points of the corner from turning through properly. Trim the excess at an angle to a point a couple of threads' width away from the stitched corner. Use a pair of tweezers to work the corner through, being careful not to stretch the fabric.

SEWING A CURVED SEAM

Echoing the form of the body, many of the structural seams of a garment are curved, creating contours such as that of the princess line, which takes in bust, waist and hip shaping. Curved seams incorporate two parts: a concave-curved section, and a convex-curved insert. Before sewing, pieces should be notched correctly at intervals for ease of insertion. To sew a curved seam:

Place the concave piece right sides up on the machine.

Matching the stitching lines, place the convex piece on top, right side down. Start stitching.

When the curved sections start to diverge, manipulate the concave section to follow the under-section, while keeping this bottom section flat. Although the stitching lines are the same length, the seam edge of the convex curve is longer than the concave. The idea when stitching is to make the concave section fit the shape of the convex section; because of this, the concave edge will frill slightly when stitched. Lowering the stitch length gives greater control when stitching the curve, and a smoother finished seam.

open seam and clipped SA, WS

On curved seams, the seam allowances should be graded. Clipping into the seam allowances of inwards (concave) curved seams by 4–7mm (³⁄₁₆–⁵⁄₁₆in) at intervals of 2.5–4cm (1–1½in) can help the seam to open up and lay flat. Notching (not to be confused with pattern notching) – where small triangular sections are clipped out from the seam allowances – can be used on outwards (convex) curves. This notching helps remove some of the bulk. Never clip completely to the seam, as this can weaken the seam and lead to the desired curve becoming angular.

THE BASICS
Fundamentals of a garment

FRENCH SEAM

A French seam is a self-neatening seam, originating from the couture ateliers.
It is commonly used on very sheer fabrics such as chiffon, fine cotton and voile.
As it uses two lines of stitching, it is also suitable for garments that receive
heavy wear, such as nightwear. Due to the extra processes required, the seam
is rare within mass industry. It is not recommended for very curved seams.
To sew a French seam:

With 1.2cm (½in) seam allowances, place sections wrong sides together with stitch lines matching. Stitch a seam 6mm (¼in) in from the seam edge and trim back to 3mm (⅛in).

Press the seam allowances open, and then fold the seam right sides together.

Stitch another line 6mm (¼in) in from the edge. Open the finished seam and press to one side.

FLAT-FELLED SEAM

This is one of the most hardwearing seams. It is suitable for all fabrics,
but is especially common for jeans and heavy cottons. It is a self-neatening
seam, where all the raw edges are enclosed, and lends itself to reversible
garments and sportswear. A flat-felled seam is constructed from two pieces
with differing seam allowances: one has a 6mm (¼in) seam allowance,
and the other has a 2cm (¾in) seam allowance that folds around the shorter,
to conceal it. To sew a flat-felled seam:

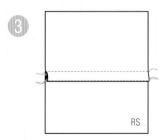

Place the wrong sides together with stitch lines matching; sew along the stitch line.

Press out the seam and fold in the longer edge (right sides together) by 6mm (¼in) and press, enclosing the raw edge of the shorter seam allowance. Edge-stitch this folded edge down.

Twin lines of stitching should show from the right side and one row of stitching from the wrong side.

WELT SEAM

The welt seam is very similar in use to a flat-felled seam. It is suitable for medium to heavy fabrics, such as wools, denims and tweeds. It creates a raised effect, and because of the twin stitch is very durable. A welt seam uses two pieces with different seam allowances, one with 6mm (¼in) and the other with 1.2cm (½in). If the piece is not lined, the longer seam allowance must be overlocked before it is sewn down. To sew a welt seam:

Neaten one edge with a wider seam allowance and place pieces right sides together with stitch lines matching; sew down the stitch line.

Press the seam, folding the overlocked edge over to cover the shorter raw edge. Turn the fabric to the right side and topstitch so that the longer seam allowance is caught on the underside and the raw edge is enclosed.

A completed welt seam from the right side. This finish gives a distinctive raised appearance, as seen with welt pockets.

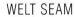

1. Panelled skirt with external seam detailing.

(Photo credit: Bon Marché)

THE BASICS
Fundamentals of a garment

BOUND SEAM

Binding is a way of finishing that encloses the raw fabric edge with a strip of bias-cut fabric, which can be either in the self-fabric or a contrast material. It is a suitable finish for many fabrics, but is often seen in unlined outerwear. Machine feet with binding attachments can be bought for industrial and domestic machines and cut the following steps down to one process. To sew a bound closed seam:

plain seam, closed, WS

Sew a plain seam (see p. 19) and press the seam allowances to one side.

To sew a bound open seam:

fold
fold
fold
grainline

Take two garment sections with 1.2cm (½in) seam allowances. Cut a bias fabric strip for the binding to the length required and 4cm (1½in) wide; this allows for the strip becoming narrower as it is sewn. Press the binding strip into four equal sections along its length or use a bias-binding maker if available.

RS

Fold the binding strip onto the wrong side, so that it encloses the raw edge. Press. From the right side, edge-stitch the folded edge on the wrong side.

closed seam, WS

Bind using method below.

RS

Sew the strip onto one of the garment sections right sides together along the pressed crease line.

open seam, WS

Repeat for the other side. Sew together the sections as plain seam (see p. 19).

see p. 19

NOTCHES

Notches are clipped markers in the seam allowances of paper pattern pieces. Pattern notchers are used for making them. These notches are transferred onto fabric as a chalk line or a small (3mm/⅛in) snip. Notches can also be made by snipping a small triangle into the edge of the pattern.

Notches denote important positions such as the waistline, hip line, pleats or darts. They help to indicate match points on complicated seams, such as highly curved seams where the lengths of seam edges of concave and convex curves can differ greatly. As a rule, notches should be placed in the middle of a long section to ensure that garment parts do not stretch while being sewn.

Notches provide essential markers for pattern cutters and machinists. For pattern cutters, they can indicate garment balance. The balance, or pitch points, on sleeves ensure that the sleeve falls correctly and does not twist when inset. For the machinist, notches enable pieces to be matched up accurately, and allow fullness to be allocated precisely in areas with tolerance (ease).

PIPED SEAM

A piped seam is an ornamental seam, used to enhance style lines. It can be used with many fabrics, but thinner to medium-weight materials are best used for the piping casing, as thicker fabrics may be too bulky. For an alternative look, the cord can be removed once the seam has been stitched. To sew a piped seam:

Use a 1.2cm (½in) seam allowance on seam sections. Cut a bias strip of fabric for the binding 3cm (1¼in) wide for the length needed, plus a small amount extra.

Fold the bias strips in half, wrong sides together, enclosing a length of cord against the folded edge.

With the zipper foot attached, sew a line of stitching close to the piping.

Matching the seam edges, sew the piping right side together to one of the garment sections with the same zipper foot along the same line.

Attach the other garment section as before and press seams outwards.

Piped seam from the wrong side.

Piped seam from the right side.

THE BASICS
Fundamentals of a garment

DARTS

Darts provide a three-dimensional structure to a garment. They suppress volume that may be required in one section of a garment, but unwanted elsewhere. Traditional areas for dart shaping are the bust, chest, waist and hips – all areas that contour the natural body shape. However, darts can be applied anywhere in a garment that the design dictates, such as on a sleevehead to provide extra fullness. Darts can be a necessity to provide shape, but this does not mean that they have to be boring or ugly; a well-placed dart can enhance the lines of a design.

In the industry, darts are marked by a drill hole inset to a set distance (i.e.,1.2cm/½in from the apex of the dart and 3mm/⅛in from the width), but tailor's tacks or a chalk mark are equally sufficient.

While stitching a dart, it is possible to back-tack in order to secure the stitch at the apex. However, in certain instances this can be bulky, and creates a bump when pressed. For the following methods of dart construction, backstitching is not used; instead, the hanging threads are tied off at the tip of the dart. This technique is more time-consuming but gives a cleaner finish.

When a dart is pattern-cut, the dart lines are marked with straight lines. However, most darts need to be curved off, or contoured, when stitching, to produce a naturalistic body shape. These curves can be either concave (inwards), or convex (outwards), depending on the area of shaping.

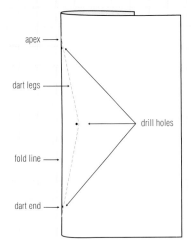

apex

dart legs

drill holes

fold line

dart end

stitch direction

concave dart

BASIC WEDGE DART

To construct a basic wedge dart, fold the dart in half, right sides together, along the fold line up to the apex, matching the notches of the dart at the seam allowances. Stitch along the dart line, dropping down to a smaller stitch length when 1.2cm (½in) from the apex. Without backstitching, sew off the edge of the folded fabric from the apex, leaving threads. Tie off the loose threads into a knot, and trim. Wedge darts can be straight, concave or convex; we have illustrated a concave dart only.

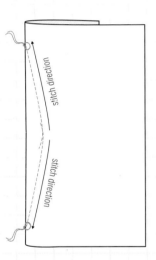

stitch direction

stitch direction

CONTOUR DARTS

Contour or 'fisheye' darts are diamond-shaped rather than triangular wedges. They shape the body from bust through waist to hip, but can be used elsewhere. To construct, mark off drill holes at dart apexes and dart widths; fold in half along the fold line, with right sides together. Stitch from the centre of the dart to the apexes at either end, knotting threads at both points. To stop the dart from pinching at the centre, slightly curve off the angle at the widest part of the dart when stitching.

TRIMMING DARTS

Some darts, such as at the waist on a tailored jacket, need to be trimmed back and opened up so they lay flat from the right side. However, there are other instances, such as for sheer fabrics, or with large and bulky darts, where darts are best trimmed down. Here, sew another line of stitching 3mm (⅛in) in from the original stitch line. Overlock off the excess up to this new edge.

CURVED/SHAPED DARTS

To construct curved or shaped darts:

DECORATIVE DARTS

To enhance shaping, darts can
be topstitched, and even reversed
so that the dart is on show
(see Basic wedge dart, p. 27).

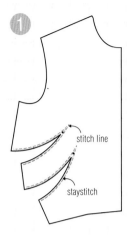

①

stitch line

staystitch

Prepare by marking off drill holes onto
fabric. To stop the dart from stretching,
staystitch 3mm (⅛in) in from dart
stitch line.

②

clip SA

Fold through the centre line, and
stitch the dart line as for wedge darts.
Clip into the dart to allow it to lay flat
as a curve.

DART TUCKS

Dart tucks are darts that are stitched only partway to the apex, allowing the fullness to be released at
a specific point; once pressed, these may look like an inverted pleat or knife pleat, depending on how
the dart is pressed. For a knife pleat, the dart is pressed cleanly to one side; for an inverted pleat, the
dart amount is pressed flat equally on either side of the stitch line.

①

Centre
FRONT
cut 1
on fold

Mark drill holes on the pattern just
inside the stitch line to ensure that
marking does not show after the
dart is sewn.

②

Prepare by marking off drill holes onto
the fabric. Fold fabric along centre of
dart and stitch outside drill holes.

③

*inverted
pleat*

*knife
pleat*

Lightly press the finished dart tuck.
Any dart excess can be pressed cleanly
to one side or divided equally either
side of the stitch line.

PRESSING DARTS

Press each dart as soon as it has been constructed. Horizontal darts are generally pressed downwards, and vertical darts towards the centre front or centre back.

REINFORCED DARTS

Reinforced darts can be produced by stitching off from the apex onto a small piece of fabric; this negates the need to backstitch and is more secure than just knotting off the thread ends. This is a common method in tailoring, as it provides a flat appearance, but is also suitable for fine fabrics that are prone to fraying, such as organza, voile and fine cotton lawns. To construct reinforced darts:

Bias-cut a small piece of fabric 4 x 4cm (1½ x 1½in). Fuse, if required. Fold in half and place the folded edge at the end of the dart, with the apex of the dart at the centre of the piece. Sew the dart as normal, stitching off from the tip onto the reinforcing fabric section. Cut through the folded dart up to the attached fabric.

Clip into the dart at this point so that the dart tip can be pressed to one side.

Trim around the excess of the reinforcing fabric to the shape of the tip, leaving a rounded amount around the point of the dart.

Open out the reinforcing section.

Snip as shown; this helps keep the tip flat when pressed.

Press the dart open.

THE BASICS
Fundamentals of a garment

CHAPTER 3: FABRIC CONSIDERATIONS

INTERFACINGS

There are many ways to add body and weight to a material, helping it to hold its shape. Most methods use other fabrics as support. These interfacings can either be sewn in place, for instance as a canvas to support the front of a tailored jacket, or fused onto the wrong side of the fabric.

TYPES OF INTERFACING

A wide array of interfacings are available, each with different properties that are suitable for various fabrics and uses.

- **Woven interfacings:** A wide variety of weights of fabric (usually cotton), with very little give or stretch.

- **Vilene interfacing:** A brand of non-woven fabric available in a range of thicknesses, and in fusible and stitch-on versions.

- **Reinforced or staystitched interfacings:** These have fine stitch lines running in one or two directions that support in their specified direction. They're often used across a pocket on a jacket to stop it stretching.

- **Stretch fusibles:** Ideal for stretch wovens and jersey fabrics.

- **Leather, suede and fur interfacings:** These use a glue with a low melting temperature so as not to damage the material.

- **Engineered fusings and front fusibles:** Open knitted interfacings used to add support to suitings while keeping the drape qualities of the fabric.

- **Canvas and horsehair:** Used mainly in tailoring. Made from mixes of wool, linen, hair and viscose, and available in varying weights. They offer a permanent support to areas on a jacket such as the chest, shoulder, sleevehead and collar, and are also used in corsetry and underskirts for strength and structure. Fusible canvases can also be found.

- **Crinoline:** Stiff netting used to support voluminous shapes such as full skirts.

- **Wadding/padding:** Can be used to support specific areas or a whole garment in order to change silhouette. Can also be used to add warmth in a garment.

1. Image key
a) Charcoal Vilene fusible interfacing. A non-woven fusing, available in many weights (medium-weight shown here)
b) White cotton (woven) fusible interfacing (lightweight)
c) Vilene (non-woven) fusible interfacing (lightweight)
d) Front-fusible knitted interfacing, suitable for tailoring (medium-weight)
e) Black cotton (woven) fusible interfacing (lightweight)
f) White Vilene (non-woven) fusible interfacing (medium-weight)
g) Fine fusing on a synthetic chiffon base (very lightweight)

(Suppliers: Eastman Staples Limited, Vena Cava Design, Kleins, MacCulloch & Wallis)

FUSIBLE INTERFACING

Fusible interfacing uses a heat-reactive, meltable glue, which is sprayed thinly and evenly over the interfacing, or 'printed' on with glue dots. The fusing is then affixed to the fabric using an iron. Do not use a steam setting as this can prevent the fusing from adhering correctly. It is important that the correct temperature and time of fusing is achieved to prevent delamination, whereby the layers of self and fusing come apart. Over time, with use and washing, this may still happen; certain companies will not use fusibles for this reason.

When using fusibles, care must be taken that the glue does not come through onto the right side of the fabric; this is called strike-through. Strike-back, conversely, is where the glue seeps through to the back of the interfacing. For transparent or very thin fabrics, a layer of organza or organdy of the same colour can be sewn in to give 'invisible' added structure. Alternatively, an extra middle layer of the self-fabric, such as crepe georgette for a collar, can be used for a softer support; this may be more suited to the desired feel and look of the end garment.

When fusing, sections within the body of the garment traditionally call for a supple, flexible interfacing, whereas areas around the profile edge, such as the collar, rever, hem and cuff, need stiffer support in order to prevent warping over time. Test the fusing beforehand on your fabric; it should enhance the fabric, without hardening or looking obviously fused.

THE BASICS
Fabric considerations

OTHER FORMS OF SUPPORT

As well as interfacings there are other materials that can be used
to support fabric to create a specific shape or silhouette that would
not be formed naturally.

BONING

Boning was traditionally used in the making of corsetry, whereby reshaped
whalebones were stitched into channels within the garment to attain a desired
body support and silhouette. Today, products such as Rigilene, made of a series
of polyester rods woven together, and plastic boning are available to give the
same effect. Metal boning has the added bonus of being able to curve both
vertically and horizontally, and therefore better contours to the body. This
metal boning can be shortened, but less easily than Rigilene; metal boning
has rounded ends that protect the wearer, and must be taken off and
reattached to shorten. When shortening Rigilene, it is best to curve off the
cut ends or protect the wearer by stitching over a soft fabric such as velvet.

Boning can either be attached to the wrong side of the self-fabric or lining
for a decorative finish (this will give visible topstitching), or applied to an
interfacing of canvas or cotton. This interfacing is layered between the self and
the lining, and provides an invisible support. Rigilene can be positioned in place
and stitched through; metal boning must be inserted into a channel sewn into
the garment.

SHOULDER PADS

These come in a wide range of styles and applications, from tailored to raglan.
Pads can be custom made to create a specific shape by layering wadding to
the desired thickness and placing it between two pieces of calico. Use large
stitches to secure the layers together.

1. A bustier dress. Strapless
garments often include a boned
bodice for additional support.
(Photo credit: Fever)

2. Image key
a) Twill-covered boning
b) Spiral wire (to be cut to size)
c) Spiral wire end caps
d) Synthetic whalebone

(Suppliers: Eastman Staples Limited, Vena Cava
Design, Kleins, MacCulloch & Wallis)

3. Image key

a) Set-in, tailored shoulder pad
(for jackets)

b) Raglan shoulder pad (multiple
use, primarily garments with raglan
or kimono-style sleeves)

c) Women's medium tailored
shoulder pad (for jackets and
soft tailoring)

d) Small fabric-covered foam
shoulder pad (multiple uses:
soft tailoring, tops and blouses)

(Suppliers: Eastman Staples Limited,
Kleins, MacCulloch & Wallis)

LAYOUT, CUTTING AND MARKING

Care and attention paid during the layout, cutting and marking stage
of garment manufacture ensures your garment achieves not only the best
possible fit and appearance, but also the most economical use of fabric.

GRAIN

The different characteristics of a fabric's grain play an important part in
how a garment will look. Incorrect cutting can twist the garment and spoil
its appearance; however, once the qualities of grain are understood they
can be utilised to great effect.

The grain denotes the direction of threads within a woven fabric. The warp
threads, or straight grain, run parallel with the selvedge; the weft threads,
or crossgrain, run across the fabric, at right angles to the selvedge.

The warp threads run continuously down the fabric. They are very stable
and provide strength while the fabric is being woven. Weft threads form
the weaving pattern and tend to be more elastic than the warp. Even more
elastic is the bias of the fabric, which may run at any angle diagonal to the
warp and weft. A true bias is at an exact 45-degree angle to the warp and
has the greatest amount of give.

Binding strips for seam edges and piping are both cut on this bias line;
being bias-cut it easily follows and forms around any curves without
distorting the seam. Bias cutting exploits this natural stretch and is often
used to create garments that form to the body and fall and drape softly,
though this often requires generous amounts of cloth when laying out.
Bias cutting lends itself to eveningwear and lingerie.

COMMON GRAINLINES FOR MAIN PATTERN PIECES

Fronts – Parallel to CF.

Backs – Parallel to CB.

Sleeves – On the centre line, which can be attained by folding sleeve in half, matching together underarm seams.

Top collars – On CB.

Undercollars – Bias cut or on CB, depending on the look desired. Bias will achieve softer results than a top and undercollar both cut on the CB straight grain.

Lapel facings – Parallel to CF, generally in line with the lapel edge.

Traditional shirt yokes and collars – Crossgrain to utilise warp strength.

Waistbands – Crossgrain to utilise warp strength.

Trouser legs – On the centre line, which can be attained by folding the trouser leg in half and matching inside and outer leg seams together.

Patch pockets – Should be derived from the grainline of the piece it is located on. Pay attention to pattern and stripes, as pockets can be cut to either blend into or contrast with the garment section to which they are attached.

1. This striped shirt utilises panels with contrasting grain direction.

(Photo credit: ASOS)

FABRICS WITHOUT GRAIN

Knitted fabrics such as jersey have no thread direction; however, they must be treated as if they do, using the wales or ribs (lengthwise columns of loops) as the straight grain and courses (knitted rows) as the crossgrain.

Felts and some other non-woven fabrics, such as Tyvek, rubber and leather, have no grain, and can be cut in any direction. Due to the nature of their construction, these fabrics do not fray in the same manner as wovens.

IDENTIFYING GRAIN

fold

selvedge

SLEEVE cut 1 pair

use a tape measure or a dressmaker's ruler to check that pattern pieces are aligned correctly with the grain of the fabric

CF

CF

UNDERCOLLAR

CB

FRONT cut 1 pair
self

CUFF cut 1 pair

CHECKING AND STRAIGHTENING GRAIN

As fabrics can be distorted out of shape in handling at the textile mill, it is important to check that the warp and weft threads within your fabric are at perfect right angles.

To check the grain, pull on a weft thread at the edge of your fabric length and cut across; if this newly cut edge is not at 90 degrees to the selvedge, it will be necessary to straighten the fabric. If marginally off-grain, fold the fabric right sides together, matching and pinning selvedge edges every 12cm (5in) or so and press; this will realign the weft threads. If the fabric is considerably off-grain, grasp the fabric at the sides and pull across the bias until the right angle between warp and weft is created.

Immersing fabric in warm water beforehand can help to relax fibres; check that the fabric is washable prior to doing so. Fabric that cannot be pulled into shape should be pressed into shape; distortion may not show when the pattern piece is flat but once constructed it will be evident, and impossible to rectify.

PREPARING FABRIC

Depending on the fabric used, you may need to follow certain preparatory methods before it can be cut. Most natural fabrics, apart from silks, will need shrinking, if not already pre-shrunk by the manufacturer. The most common way to do this is to steam-press the fabric. Alternatively, you can fold the fabric and immerse it in a basin of hot water for 30–60 minutes. The fabric can then be removed, lightly wrung out and dried. Laundering or dry cleaning the fabric can also produce the same effect. Synthetic fabrics will not shrink, but pressing without steam will help to remove creases.

Bolts of patterned fabric.

(Photo credit: Ryann Ford)

RIGHT AND WRONG SIDES OF FABRIC

Determining the right and wrong sides of fabric is not always easy, especially if both fabric surfaces are similar. With fabric bought on a roll, the right side typically faces in to protect it from damage. Needle holes on the selvedge can also help determine the correct side. On the right side the holes should puncture through, leaving a slightly raised exit on the wrong side. Slubs and imperfections on the wrong side may be evident; the right side may also have a sheen, or particular finish, that differs from the underside. Ultimately, using the right or wrong side is a design choice; your preferred side should be chosen as the 'right' side.

PATTERN AND PRINT

When patterning with printed fabric, carefully observe pattern direction and ensure that you lay your pieces onto the fabric for cutting according to its individual properties.

- One-way patterns have a dominant design direction, which means that all pieces must be positioned and cut in the same direction.

- Two-way patterns, such as small, busy floral prints, have a specific direction, but one that is not so significant as to warrant one-way-only positioning.

- Non-directional patterns, such as polka dots, stripes or checks, have no specific direction and can be positioned (if the pile allows) in opposite directions.

- Fabrics with border prints, such as for a skirt hem, are often cut on the crossgrain so that the border runs horizontally across the garment.

1. Image key
a, b, e, f) Non-directional pattern
c) One-way pattern
d, g) Two-way pattern
Suppliers: Husqvarna Studio (Bath)

PILE DIRECTION

The pile or nap of cloth denotes the direction or lay of the surface fibres on the fabric. These can be divided into two types.

- One-way pile fabrics have a prominent pile that lays in a single direction. Corduroy, suede, fur and velvet are examples. All pattern pieces must be cut following this direction, which can cause significant fabric waste.

- Two-way pile fabrics have a small pile and allow for positioning sections in opposite directions. This tends to create less waste than one-way pile fabrics.

- Although not technically a napped surface, fabrics such as moiré (watermarked) taffeta or satin reflect light differently depending on the angle; once the desired direction is chosen all pieces must be cut in that direction. This is even more applicable for two-tone fabrics.

Fabric with a pile or directional print needs to be laid out to ensure all pieces lie in the same direction in the finished garment

THE BASICS
Fabric considerations

SYMMETRY

Most garments have a symmetrical nature, and it is important that stripes, tartans, checks and prints are cut so that the parts from either side of the garment mirror one another. There are two forms of both: even checks and balanced stripes that repeat symmetrically in either direction, and uneven checks and unbalanced stripes that do not.

Always cut striped or checked pieces individually, marking stripe locations on the edge of the pattern so they can be matched exactly for the opposite, adjoining piece. To achieve a professional look, match horizontal stripes or checked patterns at vertical seams such as the centre front and back and side seams. Sleeves should also be cut so that the pattern continues visually at the same height around the garment.

LAYING OUT A PATTERN

The majority of garment pieces are cut on the warp/straight grain; the direction of this grain will be marked clearly on the pattern. To ensure that the grain is precise, each pattern piece should be measured from the selvedge to the grainline on the pattern with a ruler or tape measure, checking that each end of the pattern piece is the same distance from the edge. (See diagram on p. 36.)

Care must be taken to cut with the grain as much as possible. Pressing and sewing must also be done with the grain so as not to distort or stretch the fabric. On any bias edges, a line of staystitching 3mm (⅛in) from the edge will help to stop the piece from stretching, which distorts both length and width. Fusible bias stay tape can also be used for the same result.

THE LAYOUT

In order to produce a garment cost-effectively, pattern pieces must be economically arranged according to grainline, pile direction and pattern of the fabric. In mass production, this layout is created by pattern-making software so as to limit fabric waste and reduce costs. Most manufacturers aim for at least 80–85 per cent efficiency of fabric use. A layout will be made for each fabric used within a garment, including interfacings.

See diagram on p. 36.

TIPS ON CUTTING FINE FABRIC

To stabilise fine fabrics such as chiffon when cutting, place a sheet of pattern paper underneath, pinning through both layers to add support, and cut through all layers.

Use low-tack masking tape to stick fine or drapey fabrics to the edge of the table. This will make it easier to obtain a straight selvedge and stop warping, and ensure that the pattern pieces can be cut on a straight grain.

Do not try to speed up the process by doubling the fabric; cut pattern pieces from a single layer.

Although suitable for a wide variety of fabrics, rotary cutters can be especially handy for finer fabrics. Since they use pressure from above, they are less likely to stretch or shift the material when cutting.

1. A symmetrical print layout is used to great effect in this monochrome waterfall-front cardigan.
(Photo credit: Apricot)

MARKING

Paper patterns can simply be pinned directly to or weighed down (by pattern weights) onto the pressed fabric, and then cut around. Alternatively, a sharp tailor's chalk can be used to mark around the pattern, marking all relevant pointers such as notches, darts and buttonhole placements.

For finer fabrics, or fabrics on which chalk will not show, tailor tacks or thread marks can be used. These are sewn by hand with a doubled thread and either sewn through once and then loosely knotted or sewn through twice and left. These threads are precise, able to be seen on both sides of fabric, and more permanent than chalk marks; they can be easily removed once their purpose has been served.

On a more industrial scale, drill holes are marked by laser or hole punch to position darts, the marks for which will be set in 6mm (¼in) from the dart ends. Other marking tools, such as air-erasable pens, can be used, but need to be tested for suitability on the fabric beforehand.

①

CUTTING

Most of the hard work in cutting out is in its preparation, ensuring that all pattern pieces have been laid correctly with the grain and marked with all relevant points. From then on, all you need is a sharp pair of shears and a focused eye. However, here are some pointers that can make the process easier.

Use a pair of scissors or shears that feels comfortable in the hand. Large tailor's shears, although weighty, are supported by the table surface; the cutter guides, rather than holds, the shears. Large scissors can be used with as much precision as small ones, if used with care. Separate shears should be kept for paper and fabric; cutting paper dulls the blade, which can then damage fabric when cutting.

Do not cut against yourself; position your body into the cut line, and cut with rather than into the grain. Turn sections to make it easier, and always keep sections flat when cutting. Use the point of the scissors to clip into notches.

THE BASICS
Fabric considerations

ORDER OF MAKE

Once you have cut out and fused all the relevant sections, lay out the pieces into the basic shape of the garment to check that you have all parts, and that each piece is cut correctly – that is, the right way up, with the pattern or nap in the same direction and so on.

To make the construction process swift and efficient, position pieces in the right sequence for manufacture, ordering pattern pieces by size, with larger pieces at the bottom, smaller on top, and symmetrical pieces placed right sides together. Keep any trimmings, threads and buttons with the garment pieces so they are close at hand.

Divide into sections for order of make (see pp. 44–45). Decide whether you need to sew a complicated pocket or put together an intricate section first. Some processes such as plackets, button stands, pockets and zips need to be completed or sewn when the piece is flat. Parts such as collars and neck facings should be attached as soon as the fewest necessary seams have been joined, and while the garment is still flat (i.e. side seams not sewn), as it is much easier to handle at this stage.

While sewing, continually check the seam and, if needed, unpick and correct any errors that have occurred. Do not cut corners, as doing so will result in sloppy effects that will undoubtedly show in the final piece. Once a section has been completed, it should be pressed and, if required, neatened and topstitched before moving on to the next step.

Try to simplify handling; control fabric layers by tacking them together in stages of two layers at a time – a gathered section onto an interfacing, or layers of frills and flounces. This helps to support each layer; the staystitching acts as seam reinforcement, and the section can be treated as one. Arrange the final closing procedure so as to enhance design; a shirt may be closed by French seaming the underarm/side seam, which is both functional and aesthetic.

Bear in mind that these are only guidelines; a creative and unconventional approach to the order of make is good if it will achieve a better or more appropriate result – idiosyncratic design elements may dictate this.

ARRANGEMENT OF ORDER

Whether on a small or an industrial scale, garment construction can
be simplified by ordering the assembly into separate processes.

ASSEMBLING

Assembling processes include off processes and in processes. Off processes
concern garment parts that may be constructed separately to the main body,
such as cuffs, collars and belts. In processes are construction processes that
are integral to a piece, and must be done before attaching as part of the
garment, such as darts, plackets, pockets and zips.

LINKING

Linking processes involve the joining together of main garment parts, such
as attaching the collar to the body of the garment and insetting sleeves.

CLOSING

Closing processes involve the construction of seams – such as the underarm
seam on a sleeve or the side seams on a skirt or bodice – that transform the
section from flat to three-dimensional or 'tubular'. Attaching a lining would
also be considered a closing procedure.

FINISHING

Finishing processes consist of in processes and out processes. In processes
are finishings that are made when the garment is still in sections, such as seam
neatening, overlocking and buttonholes. Out processes are finishings that
can be done only when the garment is complete, such as attaching closures
and hemming.

1. Double-breasted cape with
decorative topstitching and
domed buttons.
(Photo credit: French Connection)

2. Crested jacket. An unusual
button stand can provide an
interesting design feature on
a classic garment.
(Photo credit: La Redoute)

THE BASICS
Fabric considerations

ORDER OF MAKE FOR SELECTED GARMENTS

Although every design is individual, with details that are unique to that piece, there are general guidelines that can be followed when planning the order of construction for certain garment types.

SLEEVE INSERTION: TUBULAR METHOD

Set machine to largest stitch and sew two rows of machine basting between the notches and within seam allowance (SA).

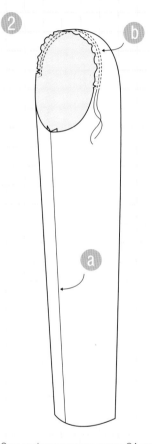

Sew underarm seam, press SA open, and turn to right side (a). Use tacking stitch to gauge tolerance (ease) in the crown, ensure fullness is distributed evenly and note how cap begins to form at shoulder (b).

open seam

match notches

sew darts

open seam

Sew darts, side and shoulder seam, and press SA open. Turn bodice to wrong side and insert tubed sleeve into armhole. Note sleeve and bodice are placed RS together. Match notches and seams, pinning sleeve at these points first. Place more pins evenly around the sleeve and tack sleeve in place, removing pins as you work. Turn bodice to RS to check fit and balance. Once satisfied with sleeve placement, turn bodice back to WS and machine into position. Ensure all seam allowances are laying flat in correct position as you sew.

BASIC SHIRT

For a basic shirt, sew the body sections first (folding and stitching the button stand before sewing darts). Leave the side seams open. Make up the collar and stand separately and attach. Construct placket on sleeve and attach sleeve to body of shirt (leaving underarm seam open). Sew up the side seam and underarm seam in one go. Attach cuff, buttons and sew buttonholes. Hem garment.

BASIC SKIRT

For a basic skirt, attach pockets, sew darts and fastenings if necessary, sew body sections of skirt (the main front and back panels), attach waistband, or, if lined, make up complete shell of lining with facings and attach. Hem.

BASIC TROUSER

For a basic trouser, attach pockets and sew fly (attaching front legs). Attach back legs at inside leg seams, then side seams. Afterwards, sew up the crotch from front to back. Attach waistband and hem garment.

LINED JACKET

For a lined jacket, first separate outer pieces from facing/lining pieces. Attach pockets and sew darts; depending on the design, you may need to sew darts before pockets. Sew main body of jacket (the main front and back sections), sew side seams and shoulder seams. Construct and attach collar, make sleeves, and inset into armholes as shown opposite. Make up lining as outer, attaching facings; sew lining to outer, bagging through sleeve. On the lining, open up part of the underarm seam in the sleeve to bag out the cuffs. This opening will be around 10cm (4in), depending on garment size/bulk, though you may need to open up more if it is difficult to pull the garment through. Once cuffs have been bagged/sewn up, sew up the opening.

1. A well-fitting jacket will have a well-made lining.

(Photo credit: Next)

THE BASICS
Fabric considerations

2

DRAFTING TECHNIQUES

CHAPTER 4: DESIGNING PATTERNS FROM SCRATCH   48
- Taking measurements   48
- Making basic blocks   50
- Pattern design essentials   56
- Dart manipulation   60
- Combining and dividing   68
- Creating your own pattern blocks   72
- Toiles   77

CHAPTER 5: FITTING PRINCIPLES AND PATTERN
ADJUSTMENTS   78

CHAPTER 6: RUB-OFF PATTERN DRAFTING   94

CHAPTER 4:
DESIGNING PATTERNS FROM SCRATCH

TAKING MEASUREMENTS

Begin by measuring the bust across the fullest part. Allow the tape to rise up 2.5cm (1in) at the centre back; if the tape drops, the measurement will decrease and the resulting block may be too tight. Compare the measurements you have with those on the chart to find those nearest in bust size and select the appropriate block; if shop-bought clothes generally fit well, you may find that the average measurements give successful results. If your measurements differ significantly from those on the chart, it may be necessary to adjust the blocks as per the fitting adjustments in Chapter 5.

NATURAL POSTURE

Ask the person you are measuring to stand naturally, looking forwards. If they don't have an upright posture, do not mask their true figure with one. Horizontal measurements can be taken snugly since varying amounts of tolerance (ease) will be added into the block.

		SMALL CM	SMALL INCHES	MEDIUM CM	MEDIUM INCHES	LARGE CM	LARGE INCHES	OWN MEASUREMENTS
①	Bust	82	$32^{1/4}$	88	$34^{5/8}$	94	37	
②	Waist	62	$24^{3/8}$	68	$26^{3/4}$	74	$29^{1/8}$	
③	High hip	74	$29^{1/8}$	80	$31^{1/2}$	86	$33^{7/8}$	
④	Hip	88	$34^{5/8}$	94	37	100	$39^{7/8}$	
⑤	Cross back	32.9	$12^{15/16}$	34.4	$13^{1/2}$	35.9	$14^{1/8}$	
⑥	Cross front	30.6	12	32.4	$12^{3/4}$	34.2	$13^{7/16}$	
⑦	Shoulder	11.8	$4^{5/8}$	12.2	$4^{3/4}$	12.6	$4^{15/16}$	
⑧	Neck size	35.5	$13^{15/16}$	37	$14^{9/16}$	38.5	$15^{1/8}$	
⑨	Bicep	27	$10^{5/8}$	28.5	$11^{1/4}$	30	$11^{13/16}$	
⑩	Wrist	15.3	6	16	$6^{1/4}$	16.7	$6^{1/2}$	
⑪	Nape to waist	40.4	$15^{7/8}$	41	$16^{1/8}$	41.6	$16^{3/8}$	
⑫	Front shoulder to waist	40.4	$15^{7/8}$	41	$16^{1/8}$	41.6	$16^{3/8}$	
⑬	Armhole	20.4	8	21	$8^{1/4}$	21.6	$8^{1/2}$	
⑭	Sleeve length	57.8	$22^{3/4}$	58.5	23	59.2	$23^{1/4}$	
⑮	Waist to knee	57.8	$22^{3/4}$	58.5	23	59.2	$23^{1/4}$	
⑯	Waist to hip	20.2	$7^{15/16}$	20.6	$8^{1/8}$	21	$8^{1/4}$	
⑰	Waist to floor	102.5	$40^{3/8}$	104	41	105.5	$41^{1/2}$	
⑱	Body rise	27	$10^{5/8}$	28	11	29	$11^{3/8}$	

DRAFTING TECHNIQUES

Designing patterns from scratch

MAKING BASIC BLOCKS

The following basic blocks (templates; also known as slopers) form the basis for most of the pattern-drafting techniques in this book. They require scaling to full size, as keyed to the images. After your blocks are scaled, it is essential to construct a toile (see p. 77) to assess fit and/or any necessary adjustments before committing this template to cardboard: refer to the fitting and alteration exercises in Chapter 5 to tailor your blocks to an individual figure or to correct faults. You may also wish to consider making a direct trace of these blocks to practise the pattern-drafting exercises throughout the book, rather than immediately jumping to full-size experimentation.

USING THIS DRESS BLOCK
The basic dress block is shown to the hip line and can be extended as required. A copy of this block can also be drawn only to the waist, which will prove useful for waisted designs.

SLEEVE BLOCK

bicep

elbow

wrist

SCALE ▢ = 2.5cm (1in)

KEY

 = SMALL   = MEDIUM = LARGE

·—·—· = CLOSE-FITTING

·—·—· = SHAPED CUFF

DRESS BLOCK

CB

bust

BACK

waist

hip

CF

bust

FRONT

waist

hip

DRAFTING TECHNIQUES

Designing patterns from scratch

SKIRT BLOCK

CB

hip

BACK

CF

hip

FRONT

1. Charlotte vintage stripe dress.

(Photo credit: Fat Face)

2. Chiffon batwing blouse.

(Photo credit: Blue Inc)

① ②

MAKING CULOTTES FROM THE SKIRT BLOCK

A culotte, or divided skirt, is a versatile fashion shape. This type of garment falls flatter from the waistline than a conventional trouser. The basic skirt block forms the starting point for this drafting process.

Trace around both front and back basic skirt blocks, ensuring you have enough room on your paper for the crotch extension. Measure the front and back blocks separately along the hip line and make a note of both figures. Once drafted, this block can be extended to the desired length and further manipulated as per the skirt. It is readily converted to styles based upon the A-line and panel skirt techniques, or connected to a bodice to create a romper.

1. This cotton romper uses a culotte skirt joined to a simple bodice with a gathered waist.

(Photo credit: Apricot)

BASIC SKIRT BLOCK

a

a–c = body rise plus 1.5cm ($^5/_8$in).

d

d = halfway between A and C.

e = half back hip measurement plus 1.5cm ($^5/_8$in). Connect d to e with a smooth curve.

e

c

BACK

CB

hip

b

b = halfway between basic skirt block hip and hem.

f

f–g = body rise plus 1.5cm ($^5/_8$in).

i

i = halfway between f and h.

j = half back hip measurement minus 1.5cm ($^5/_8$in). Connect i to j with a smooth curve.

j

h

FRONT

CF

hip

g

g = halfway between basic skirt block hip and hem.

BASIC CULOTTE BLOCK

CB

BACK

hip

CF

FRONT

hip

PATTERN DESIGN ESSENTIALS

The following techniques are essential to ensure that your finished garment has the best possible appearance, and should be undertaken after completing the draft pattern.

CHECKING THE RUN OF A PATTERN

Once the pattern-drafting process is complete, you need to ensure that the pattern pieces will work together harmoniously during construction. To check the run of a pattern:

1. Pattern pieces that will be sewn together should be laid next to each other with edges touching: check how they interact and, if necessary, draw a smooth continuous line to bridge seams. This process makes shapes easier to sew together as well as helping to avoid unsightly angles in a finished garment, a fault that can be particularly evident at side seams and on mirrored pieces cut on the fold.

2. Laying pattern pieces together before cutting out also ensures that measurement inconsistencies are noticed and corrected before time and money are wasted with easily avoided mistakes. Small differences in length between pieces can generally be evened out; simply redraw a bridging line using the half/half method: add to the shorter line, remove from the longer.

1. A dress featuring asymmetric tuck darting.

(Photo credit: Freemans)

smooth seam run

CB

CF

smooth seam run

SIDE BACK
cut 1 pair

SIDE FRONT
cut 1 pair

even out length inconsistencies

①

TRUING UP DARTS

This process ensures that the dart excess will maintain the same profile as the seam allowance after construction. To true up darts:

1. Fold pattern paper along dart legs and drop dart into position.
2. Use the tracing wheel to roll through side seam.
3. Note how the waist seam is drawn up at an angle when dart legs are closed. To compensate, fold pattern and create a smooth continuous line. Open out the pattern paper ready to add seam allowances, observing the extended profile of the dart excess between the dart legs.

① fold dart into position

ADDING SEAM ALLOWANCES

Seam allowance (SA) is added
after the completion of pattern
manipulation, as the blocks used
to create individual patterns
do not contain the necessary
fabric allowance to enable
sewing together.

Seam allowance widths vary
depending on the required finish:
A French seam requires 1.2cm
(½in) to accommodate the
double turn, whereas a plain seam
may only require a 1cm (⅜in)
allowance. Curved seams, or seams
that will be bagged out, can be
trimmed after construction to
reduce unnecessary bulk, but you
could also draft a narrower seam
allowance from the offset.

Many commercial home
dressmaker patterns include
allowances between 1.5 and 2cm
(⅝ and ¾in), building in an extra
margin of width that may be needed
when the first toile is fitted.
The first working pattern of a style
you have drafted from scratch
would also benefit from this extra
allowance, which can be trimmed
from the working pattern should
the first fitting toile prove
it unnecessary.

LOWERING THE DART APEX

Lowering the dart apex accommodates the fullness of the bust and avoids a pointed appearance in the final garment. The waist and bust dart apexes are simply shortened by 2cm (¾in) and the dart legs redrawn.

shorten darts
2cm (¾in)

CF

LOW NECKLINES

Any design with a low front or back neckline requires an additional step to remove excess tolerance (ease) through the bust and neckline. This adjustment should also be made to any style with a low rever to ensure the collar does not drag.

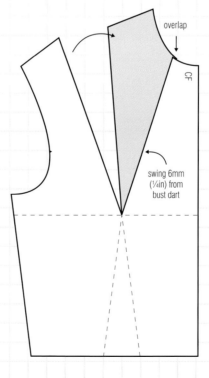

overlap

CF

swing 6mm
(¼in) from
bust dart

DART MANIPULATION

Dart manipulation is the act of transferring a dart to a new position within a pattern piece, to provide the same amount of suppression and shaping. In the following pages we will explain how to move the darts into standard positions, as well as providing further examples, such as a princess line manipulation, which hides the darts in style lines. Scaled experimentation is to be encouraged, as these positions and techniques covered are by no means exhaustive. The following methods use a basic waisted bodice block with a bust dart.

MOVING DARTS

Darts can be moved horizontally, although there are limits to this. As a general rule, darts can be moved 2cm (¾in) horizontally in either direction with very little trouble, but any more than this and the garment will begin to take on a flatter appearance and start to crease or pull at the side seams. Suppression should be spread evenly around a garment, so that a fully three-dimensional garment is achieved.

STANDARD DART POSITIONS

UNDERARM DART

Mark new dart position and cut along this line.

Pivot the released (grey) section to close the original bust dart position.

Shorten dart apex.

SHOULDER TO ARMHOLE

Mark new dart position and cut along this line.

Pivot the released (grey) section to close the original bust dart position.

Shorten dart apex.

SHOULDER TO NECKLINE

Mark new dart position and cut along this line.

Pivot the released (grey) section to close the original bust dart position.

Shorten dart apex.

DRAFTING TECHNIQUES
Designing patterns from scratch

SHOULDER TO CENTRE FRONT

Mark new dart position and cut along this line.

Pivot the released (grey) section to close the original bust dart position.

Shorten dart apex.

FRENCH DART

Mark new dart position and cut along this line.

Pivot the released (grey) section to close original bust dart position.

Cut along one of the waist dart legs.

Pivot the released (grey) section to close original waist dart position: dart excess from waist and bust dart are now contained in a single dart.

Lower dart apex.

BACK SHOULDER DART TO ARMHOLE

Mark new shoulder dart position and cut along this line; pivot the released (grey) section to close the original shoulder dart position. It is not necessary to shorten the dart apex on a shoulder dart.

BACK SHOULDER TO NECKLINE

Mark new shoulder dart position and cut along this line; pivot the released (grey) section to close the original shoulder dart position. It is not necessary to shorten the dart apex on a shoulder dart.

SHOULDER POINT

Mark new shoulder dart position and cut along this line; pivot the released (grey) section to close the original shoulder dart position. It is not necessary to shorten the dart apex on a shoulder dart.

SPLIT DART: SHOULDER DART INTO FOUR DARTS

Mark new dart positions and cut along these lines.

Fan out the released (grey) sections.

Shorten dart apex. Sewing radiating darts can prove tricky on some fabrics: consider using them in combination with dart tucks (see p. 28), as shown here.

SPLIT DART: SHOULDER AND WAIST DART INTO THREE DARTS AT WAIST

Move bust dart into waist dart. Draw 2.5cm (1in) from dart leg.

Fan out the released (grey) sections.

Lower dart apex.

DRAFTING TECHNIQUES
Designing patterns from scratch

CURVED DART

① Mark new curved dart positions and cut uppermost line.

② Pivot the released (grey) section to close the bust dart. Repeat for waist dart.

③ Darts in new position. Remember to lower the dart apex.

ASYMMETRIC DART

① Cut along both waist darts to close the bust dart.

② Draw in new dart position.

③ Cut along this line and close one waist dart.

④ The dart apex now needs to be lowered as for previous manipulation.

STYLE LINES EXPLAINED

Both a princess line and a Vienna line create shaping by transferring dart excess into seamed style lines. In the case of a princess line, the bust dart is transferred into the shoulder line; with a Vienna line, it is moved to the armhole.

STYLE LINES

Style lines are seam lines that utilise dart shaping. Within reason, these can be any shape and design. If the chosen seam intersects where the original dart is positioned, the dart can be easily transferred into the seam using the slash and spread method, as shown in diagram 1. If your style line is further away from the dart, an amount of excess from the remainder of the dart will have to be eased in, or a small dart can be created on the centre front panel. In this instance, the style line is marked and the waist darts are redrawn in line with the new panel, using as much or as little of the waist shaping as the design dictates (2). The panels are then separated (3) and a seam allowance added (4).

VIENNA LINE FRONT

DRAFTING TECHNIQUES

Designing patterns from scratch

VIENNA LINE BACK

1. Colour-panel dress with Vienna-line shaping.

(Photo credit: Heatons)

SHOULDER DART INTO BACK YOKE SEAM

PRINCESS LINE FRONT

Additional shaping for a closer fit can also be drafted at this stage.

PRINCESS LINE BACK

Additional shaping for a closer fit can also be drafted at this stage.

DRAFTING TECHNIQUES

Designing patterns from scratch

COMBINING AND DIVIDING

Where design dictates, garment sections can be combined, removing seams that would otherwise distract from the overall look. As a general rule, pattern pieces with straight edges can simply be joined, while for those with shaping, any suppression needs to be transferred to another part of the garment.

SHIRT YOKE

This technique is commonly used on traditional shirt yokes and uses both combining and dividing techniques. It is a development of the back yoke seam dart manipulation technique covered on p. 66.

Pivot shoulder dart into the armhole and connect point of dart to the CB with a dashed line. Cut along this line to release the back shoulder section.

Lay the released back shoulder section to the shoulder line of the front pattern piece, touching at the shoulder point (SP) and shoulder neck point (SNP).

Trace a new copy of the combined yoke, smoothing the seam runs at neck and shoulder to give a smooth continuous line. Add SA and pattern annotation.

1. A sleeveless shirt with
a decorative yoke.

(Photo credit: ASOS)

DECORATIVE YOKE

In this technique, a more stylised yoke shape is created using the same principles described previously. A section of both the front and back pattern is removed and joined at the shoulder seam.

Pivot shoulder dart into the armhole and connect point of dart to the CB with a dashed line. Cut along this line to release the back shoulder section.

Lay the released back shoulder section to the shoulder line of the front pattern piece, touching at SP and SNP.

Trace a new copy of the combined yoke, smoothing the seam runs at neck and shoulder to give a smooth continuous line. Add SA and pattern annotation.

DRAFTING TECHNIQUES

Designing patterns from scratch

EMPIRE LINE

An empire-line manipulation can provide an excellent basis for a variety
of styles. The dart excess in both bodice and skirt sections can be further
manipulated – consider using gathers, pleats and tucks to constrain the
fullness contained in the dart. The released lower section can be discarded
altogether and a circular or semicircular skirt shape can be drafted or draped
to fit the bodice seam.

1. An embellished one-shouldered
dress with gathered bodice and
empire line.

(Photo credit: Freemans)

2. This panelled skirt has been
given additional fullness with godet
insertions between seams.

(Photo credit: Mint Velvet)

DRESS BLOCK

Divide the block at the desired
height – note that the dividing line
is squared off from the centre line
and gently curved at the side seam.

Pivot the bust dart into the
desired position.

The side seam can be straightened and
the dart width can be trimmed from the
side seam, as shown in option 1, or the
side seam and dart shaping can be
maintained for a more fitted style.

PANELLED SKIRT

A panelled skirt can be used in conjunction with many other design features: consider the use of pleats, piping or contrasting fabrics. Alternating the grain direction, on a striped or patterned fabric, can be used to great effect with this simple skirt shape.

SKIRT BLOCK

Starting with the basic skirt block, measure the hip line and divide by three. Using this figure as a guide, square a vertical line from the waist to hem at both the CF and CB to create your new seam.

Move the front dart and one of the back darts in line with this newly created seam.

Cut along the style lines to separate your skirt into individual pieces and add 2.5cm (1in) to the side seams to give the skirt a gentle flare from the hips. Add seam allowances and pattern annotation.

DRAFTING TECHNIQUES
Designing patterns from scratch

CREATING YOUR OWN PATTERN BLOCKS

Creating your own customised pattern blocks is well worth the effort. Once you have taken the time to create your basic patterns, you can use them to make anything.

CIRCLE SKIRT

Many pattern pieces use circles as a base for their construction. Varying the grain on circular pieces can give very different results in the finished garment, depending on fabric choice: experimentation is recommended. To construct a circle, the radius must be known. To find it use the calculation:

radius = circumference ÷ 6.28.

The waistline measurement gives you the inner circumference required. For a skirt with a waist measurement of 68cm (26¾in), the inner radius will be 10.8cm (4¼in):

68cm (26¾in) ÷ 6.28 = 10.8cm (4¼in)

CALCULATING RADIUS

The circumference of a circle is the measurement around a circle; the radius is a line from the centre of the circle to its outer edge.

Radius = circumference ÷ 6.28.

1. Leather circle skirt from Principles by Ben de Lisi.

(Photo credit: Debenhams)

CIRCLE SKIRT

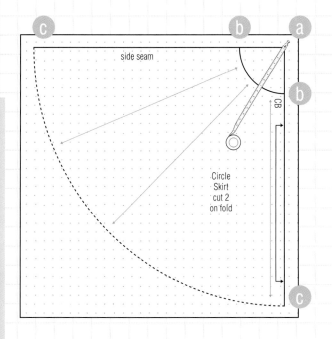

To draft a circular skirt, first calculate the radius (radius = a–b), then square off from point a. Next, draw a quarter circle to connect both points b and then draw another quarter circle from c–c: Desired skirt length = b–c.

SEMICIRCLE SKIRT

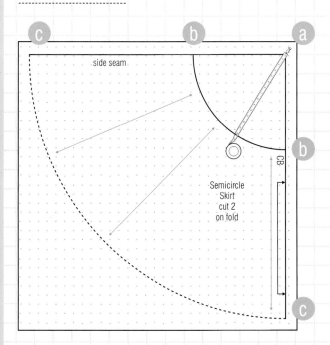

To draft a semicircular skirt, first calculate the radius (twice radius = a–b), then square off from point a. Next, draw a quarter circle to connect both points b and then draw another quarter circle from c–c: Desired skirt length = b–c.

A-LINE SKIRT

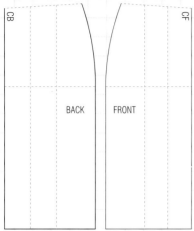

Draw a straight line connecting the waist at centre back and side seams. Divide this line by three and square a line from waist to hem to create panel seams. Repeat for front.

Back: create two 1cm x 13.5cm (⅜in x 5¼in) darts on the panel seam lines. Create another dart in the centre of these new darts measuring 2cm x 13.5cm (¾in x 5¼in). Front: create two 1cm x 10cm (⅜in x 4in) darts on the panel seam lines.

Back: slash and spread both 1cm (⅜in) darts to add volume at hem. Add 2.5cm (1in) to side seam. Repeat for front.

1. A-line skirt with scalloped layer detailing.

(Photo credit: Fever)

EASY-FIT GARMENT OR OVER-GARMENT

The basic dress block can be converted into an easy-fitting block to create garments with a more relaxed fit or as a basis for over-garments. This block can also provide an excellent basis for jersey or knitwear garments. The basic block exhibits no suppression of fullness at the waist or shaping at the side seam; this can be added as your design dictates.

EASY-FIT BODY

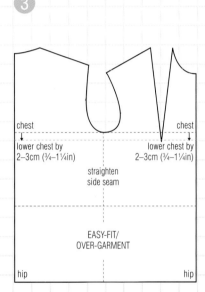

Trace around front and back blocks, leaving a gap of 5cm (2in) between side seams. Temporarily pivot bust dart from shoulder line and remove back shoulder dart width from back armhole. Squaring off from bust line, draw a dashed line vertically through front and back blocks into the centre of the shoulder line.

Raise front and back shoulder line 6mm (¼in). Slash along vertical line, opening out front and back blocks 2.5cm (1in) until side seams touch.

Lower chest line 2–3cm (¾–1¼in) on both front and back blocks and straighten side seam.

EASY-FIT SLEEVE

①

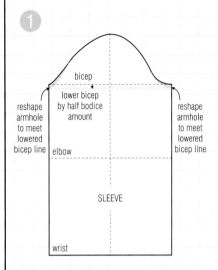

Lower bicep line by half the amount the chest line was lowered in the previous step. Reshape armhole to meet lowered bicep line.

②

Slash crown horizontally along new bicep line and then vertically through the centre line.

③

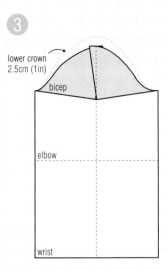

Pivot the two released crown sections downwards, lowering the crown by the same amount added through the front and back bodice. Redraw crown with a smooth continuous line.

④

Trace manipulated sleeve, creating a smooth continuous line at crown. Create a toile to check adjustments; only once you are happy with the fit of your block should it be committed to cardboard.

TOILES

A toile (derived from the French *toile*, meaning cloth), is essentially a garment prototype, sometimes also referred to as a 'muslin'; 'toile' can also be the fabric used in its creation. Up to this point, the initial pattern draft is just a hypothesis in pattern cutting, and is only proven when the toile is created and then tested on the fitting model or mannequin. In the transformation from a flat to a three-dimensional shape, many unforeseen problems can arise; the toile is a means of testing the design so that these may be corrected and the pattern resolved. It is a chance to see proportion, silhouette, style lines and design details. For these reasons, lighter-coloured fabrics are employed, as these best serve to highlight distortions in the fit of the toile.

Due to the nature of the process, the toile is often produced in calico, an inexpensive, unbleached cotton fabric, available in many qualities from lightweight muslin to heavy canvas-like weights. Primarily, the toile must be made in a fabric that behaves most similarly to the one that will eventually be used, so that the effects of weight, drape, stretch and other properties are taken into account. The toile should include any fastenings, interfacings, interlinings or understructure that would be integral to the final piece, but would not necessarily be lined or have functional pockets.

The toile should be constructed with a larger stitch length so that alterations can easily be made. Once proportion and fit have been assessed and corrected, decorative elements, such as pockets and embroidery, can be positioned.

1. Leather-trim double-breasted coat.
(Photo credit: Mint Velvet)

2. Women's jacket toile in medium-weight calico.
(Supplier: Bath Spa University)

3. Panelled culotte toile in medium-weight calico.
(Supplier: House of Jo)

DRAFTING TECHNIQUES
Designing patterns from scratch

CHAPTER 5:
FITTING PRINCIPLES AND PATTERN ADJUSTMENTS

After scaling up your blocks, the next step is to measure the block in the same positions where you have taken your measurements – bust, waist, hip, cross shoulder and so on – and compare the block to your own measurements.

It is important that you select the correct block to fit your bust and, with the following fitting techniques, tailor your block to fit an individual figure. It is advisable to copy your first block onto paper and only commit it to cardboard after you have made a bespoke block that truly fits your intended figure.

BASIC LENGTH ADJUSTMENTS

Adjustments to the length of the block can be performed by extending or overlapping across the entire width, as shown in the diagrams. The bodice block is shown with adjustments both above and below the waist, but after comparing your measurements to the block you may find only one of these adjustments is necessary, i.e., above or below the waist.

SLEEVE

overlap

overlap

Pattern adjustment position

Shorten

Lengthen

SKIRT

Pattern adjustment position   Shorten   Lengthen

BODICE

Pattern adjustment position   Shorten   Lengthen

BASIC WIDTH ADJUSTMENTS

If width alterations are being made to an existing style or pattern, the necessary width should be divided equally between all panels in the design. For specific adjustments to a dress, skirt or sleeve, follow the advice below.

BODICE

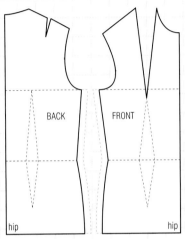

A basic width adjustment of 2.5cm (1in) or less can be made to your block side seams. If the adjustment is only required to ensure a good fit at waist or hip, only add to these sections on your block.

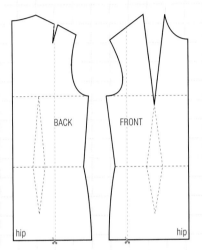

Note the scissor icons, indicating the position for pattern adjustment.

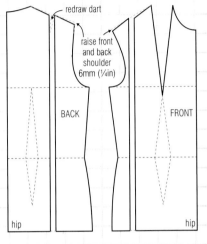

Don't add width through the neckline or armhole: this will affect the fit of your block. Divide width adjustment between front and back blocks and add through the shoulder in the case of the bodice.

SKIRT

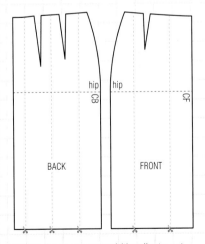

Divide the necessary width adjustment between the front and back blocks and add between the darts in the skirt block.

SLEEVE

The sleeve block is divided at the centre line to add or remove width and the crown is redrawn.

FITTING THE SHOULDERS

The following adaptations will ensure that your block sits correctly, hanging smoothly at the shoulder.

SLOPING SHOULDERS

Sloping shoulders cause the bodice and sleeve to crease unattractively at the armhole. In an over-garment or jacket, this excess may be relieved with a shoulder pad.

To correct: On both front and back pattern pieces, remove excess from the shoulder point, running to zero at the neckline. The underarm will also need to be lowered.

SQUARE SHOULDERS

Wrinkles will form across the shoulders and armhole as the toile is distorted to accommodate the breadth of the shoulders.

To correct: Slash your paper pattern as directed in the diagram and pivot the shoulder line to create more room for the shoulders. The underarm seam will also need to be raised and, as with any sleeve alteration, it will be necessary to measure the armhole to ensure compatibility with the sleeve: adjust if required.

DRAFTING TECHNIQUES
Fitting principles and pattern adjustments

NARROW SHOULDERS

The shoulders and the crown of the sleeve will drop unsupported over narrow shoulders.

To correct: Slash the pattern as shown in the diagram, and pivot the released section to remove width from the shoulder. Redraw the shoulder line.

BROAD SHOULDERS

Wrinkles at the crown and shoulder indicate that the fitting toile does not contain enough breadth for broad shoulders.

To correct: Slash the pattern as shown in the diagram, and pivot the released section to give additional fullness over the shoulder line. Redraw the shoulder line.

FITTING SLEEVELESS STYLES

Styles without a sleeve may require some adaptation to give a perfect fit.

TIGHT ARMHOLES

The armhole pulls tight and feels uncomfortable to the wearer.
To correct: Redraw the armhole to suit the individual figure, ensuring you lower the front and back by the same measurement and check the seam runs interact in a smooth manner.

LARGE ARMHOLES

The armhole is too big, exposing too much of the underarm and/or undergarments.
To correct: Redraw the armhole, raising the front and back side seams by an equal amount.

DRAFTING TECHNIQUES
Fitting principles and pattern adjustments

GAPING ARMHOLES

An armhole that gapes can be indicative of other faults within a toile: the bust could be too small or the back too large, causing excess fabric to form at the armhole. If your toile is gaping at the back armhole, refer to the alteration advice given for a wide back on p. 92 or a rounded back on p. 91. If the toile gapes at the front armhole, follow the instructions for altering the bodice for a large bust on p. 90.

BODICE BACK

BODICE FRONT

FITTING THE SLEEVES

Sleeves that are poorly fitting not only spoil the appearance of a garment but will be uncomfortable to the wearer.

INCORRECT TOLERANCE

Diagonal folds at either the front or back armhole denote incorrectly distributed tolerance (ease). This common fault is usually an error created during the construction phase, as tolerance is not correctly distributed during machining, and is not generally caused by a problem in the pattern or the block.

To correct: Unpick the sleeve and smooth the excess tolerance either to the front or back of the sleevehead as required. If wrinkles are still apparent, you may need to remove some of the tolerance from the sleevehead.

NOT ENOUGH CROWN HEIGHT

A sleeve without enough height in its crown will collapse, causing wrinkles to form as it drags across the upper arm.
To correct: Cut the crown along its top third and spread the pattern apart to add the required amount of fullness. Redraw the cap, marking a smooth line to connect the widened pattern pieces.

TOO MUCH CROWN HEIGHT

This problem will cause a furrow to appear below the cap of the sleeve.
To correct: Cut the crown along its top third, as for 'not enough crown height'. The cap should be overlapped to remove excess height. Redraw a smooth line at the crown and reposition the balance points if necessary.

DRAFTING TECHNIQUES
Fitting principles and pattern adjustments

LARGE ARM

An arm that is too large will cause your toile to pull and will feel uncomfortable to wear along most of its length.

To correct: Slash and spread both the front and back of the sleeve to add more width throughout the length of the sleeve. If this alteration does not give sufficient room for the ball of the shoulder, it may be necessary to add more height to the crown of the sleeve. The bodice will also need extra room in the armhole; pivot the released sections and redraw the armhole and dart.

SLEEVE

SLEEVE

BODICE BACK

BODICE FRONT

BODICE BACK

BODICE FRONT

TOO MUCH TOLERANCE

Excess tolerance (ease) in a sleeve will create much consternation during construction, causing unwanted wrinkles and gathering around the sleeve cap. **To correct:** Cut the sleeve horizontally along the bicep line, and separate the cap vertically into two pieces. Pivot these two pieces downwards at the centre as shown in the illustration. Redraw the cap with a smooth clean line.

THIN ARM

Excess fabric will sag and wrinkle as it drops over too narrow an arm. **To correct:** Cut the sleeve along its whole length and overlap to the desired amount. Raise the armhole on both the front and back blocks.

DRAFTING TECHNIQUES
Fitting principles and pattern adjustments

THICK ELBOW

A wide elbow will cause the sleeve to pull from the shoulder, dragging to fit the breadth of the elbow.

To correct: Cut the sleeve along its centre up to the elbow line. Pivot the released section to increase the width of the sleeve above the elbow and redraw the back seam and wrist line.

LARGE UPPER ARM

A large upper arm will cause wrinkles to concentrate in the upper portion of the arm.

To correct: Cut the sleeve along its whole length and open to the desired amount. The underarm will need to be lowered by the same amount at both the front and back side seams.

FITTING THE BUST

The following adaptations will help to correct fitting problems in the bust area.

HIGH BUST

The bust dart is positioned lower than the fullest part of the breast.
To correct: Realign the bust dart in line with the fullest part of the body.
Raise the tip of the waist dart the same amount as the bust dart has been raised.

LOW BUST

The bust dart is positioned higher than the fullest part of the breast.
To correct: Realign the bust dart in line with the fullest part of the body.
Lower the tip of the waist dart by the same amount as the bust dart has been lowered.

DRAFTING TECHNIQUES
Fitting principles and pattern adjustments

SMALL BUST

A small bust will cause the toile to collapse and crease over the bust line.
To correct: Cut your pattern piece into quarters through the centre of the waist dart and bust line. Overlap the pieces to the required amount and straighten the shoulder seam.

LARGE BUST

A large bust will cause the toile to strain across the bust line.
To correct: Cut your pattern piece into quarters through the centre of the waist dart and bust line. Spread the pieces to the required amount and redraw the waist and bust darts, noting their new increased width at the base of the dart legs.

FITTING THE BACK

The following adaptations can resolve fitting problems across the back.

VERY ERECT BACK

This causes the garment to crumple and collapse across the shoulder blades.
To correct: Assess the depth of excess fabric through the upper back and lower the centre back neckline and shoulder neck point by this amount. The shoulder point should now be raised by the same measurement.

HIGH ROUNDED BACK

This will cause the garment to pull through the shoulders and armholes.
To correct: Slash the pattern piece from the tip of the shoulder to the centre back. Raise the released section to create more length through the entire back. Cut the panel through the neckline, pivoting the shoulder until the tips of the shoulder meet. This creates a dart at the neckline. The width of this dart in relation to fabric choice dictates whether this excess can be eased or darted.

DRAFTING TECHNIQUES
Fitting principles and pattern adjustments

WIDE BACK

A toile without enough tolerance for a large back will exhibit wrinkles over the shoulders. The garment will also pull at the armholes and, unless corrected, can cause a limited range of movement for the arms.
To correct: Cut the pattern piece as directed in the diagram, moving the released section to create more breadth across the upper back. Redraw the side seam and shoulder dart, noting the wider shoulder dart position.

NARROW BACK

This will cause your toile to collapse over the shoulder blades.
To correct: Draw two lines, connecting each side of the shoulder dart to the base of the waist dart. Slash your pattern through one of these lines and overlap, pivoting slightly and obscuring both darts. This pattern piece does not now need a waist or shoulder dart, as all extra fullness has been removed.

FITTING THE HIPS

The following adaptations can greatly improve the fit at the hips and buttocks for the individual figure.

LARGE BUTTOCKS

This will cause the skirt to ride up at both the hem and waist, distorting the side seams as the toile creeps up over the buttocks.
To correct: Release the darts, allowing the centre back waist to drop to a natural position. Re-pin the darts to fit the body profile. Transfer the changes to your paper pattern, raising the waistline and adding width at the side seam to fit.

FITTING A LARGE ABDOMEN

A large abdomen will cause the skirt to ride up at both the hem and waist. Side seams will begin to skew forwards as the skirt pulls up across the hips to accommodate the abdomen.
To correct: Unpick the darts to release the centre front waist. Pin the darts to fit the shape of the waist and transfer the alterations to your paper pattern, adding to the side seams if necessary.

CHAPTER 6: RUB-OFF PATTERN DRAFTING

Although it is not widely publicised, rub-off pattern drafting, in which a pattern is traced or 'lifted' from an existing item of clothing, is not uncommon within the fashion industry. This can be fuelled by a desire to recreate a vintage find – the like of which is a staple of many design ranges.

There are two main methods of taking a pattern from an existing garment: the flat method, for predominantly flat garments, and the drape method, for more three-dimensional garments. For both methods, when all sections are traced, double-check seam lengths with the measurements of the original garment. A vintage piece is likely to have distorted with wear, so patterns should be trued up and then tested by producing a toile.

THE FLAT METHOD

For mainly flat garments, such as a skirt, the simplest approach is to trace through the item directly onto pattern paper using a spiked tracing wheel. There are likely to be areas of suppression (darts, gathering, tolerance/ease) within the garment that are slightly harder to transfer as they do not lay completely flat when pinned to paper. These may need to be estimated. If the piece can be unpicked to its component parts, the process becomes much simpler. For symmetrical garments, it is wise to trace just one half of the front and back; the piece can then be mirrored when cut. For demonstration purposes, the illustrations in this chapter show the pieces being traced on both sides.

FLAT METHOD: RUB-OFF SKIRT

Cut a piece of pattern paper the length of the skirt plus an amount extra. In the centre, mark a line straight down (CF); at about 30cm (12in) from the top, square across the hip line.

Find the CF of the skirt by measuring across and halving the amount, marking it with pins. Do this at spaced intervals down the top. If the skirt is symmetrical, you can measure from the seams rather than the edge.

To find the hip line, put the skirt on the stand (or yourself) and pin a horizontal line at the widest part of the hip. This measurement should be around 21cm (8¼in) down from the waist.

Place skirt on paper, matching CF and hip lines. Pin as flat as possible; areas that do not lie flat will have some form of shaping suppression. Trace around edge (side seams, hem and waistline) with a pencil.

DRAFTING TECHNIQUES
Rub-off pattern drafting

With a tracing wheel, trace through the seam at the waistline and central panel. Feel through to find seams of areas that may be covered by pockets, then trace through the pockets.

To find the shaping in the seam, on one side only, place a pin or drawing pin where the seam meets the hip line. Release the other side by taking out pins, then remove the pins above the hip line on both sides. Pivot so that the second panel lays flat. Pin this layer down and trace the new line.

To find the dart shaping, move the drawing pin to where the dart hits the hip line and pivot so that the other top half of the second panel lays flat. Pin this layer down and trace a new line. Draw in a new side seam from waist to hip.

Unpin the skirt from the paper to reveal your trace markings. At this stage it is important that all lines are trued up and that right angles are correct. Curves should look good and flow without bumps. Trace the lines to the other side.

9

Trace all sections. Apart from the waistband, add seam allowances, notches and hem returns (if applicable) to all skirt panels. Include grainlines and pattern annotation on each piece.

10

Repeat steps 1–9 for the back of the skirt. Make sure that connecting seams, such as the side seams, measure the same, allowing for tolerance and fullness that may be present. If not, true them up, referring back to the garment if needed.

11

Create the waistband by attaching together the front and back sections, so that the opening is on the LHS. Mirror the section on the top edge, to create a folded waistband (this is only possible for straight waistbands; for curved waistbands, cut a pair). Add seam allowances.

12

Create front and back hem facings using the traced panels, measuring the facing depth on the skirt. Add seam allowance.

DRAFTING TECHNIQUES
Rub-off pattern drafting

THE DRAPE METHOD

This technique is good for more complicated three-dimensional structures such as tailored jackets. Here, with the garment on a mannequin, fabric is used to accurately copy the pattern sections. Being fabric, it is easier to mould it to the garment shape, and areas with precise shaping can be repeated. This is particularly helpful for areas with considerable tolerance (ease), such as sleeveheads. The end result of this method is a toile shell over the existing article. Once taken apart, the final pattern can be traced onto paper.

DRAPE METHOD: RUB-OFF JACKET

1

2

Put the jacket on the tailor's dummy or stand. Fasten the jacket, and flip the collar and rever up. With pins, around the garment mark the bust line (at the fullest point of the bust), the waistline, the CF and CB.

Cut a piece of fabric the length of the jacket and around 76cm (30in) wide, or big enough to create the front panel, plus an amount extra. At around 20cm (8in) in from the LHS, draw a vertical line parallel to the grain; this is the CF. At a point 30cm (12in) down from the top of this line, square across the bust line. Measure the distance between the bust line and waistline on the jacket and mark a horizontal line at this point.

③

Place the cloth on the jacket, matching at the CF and bust line. Pin in place up CF and across bust line from the edge of the rever to the first seam/panel line.

④

Pin waistline to first seam/panel line, smoothing out excess fabric. Smooth the cloth from bust to shoulder and pin the shoulder line at both neck and arm points. Draw in the shoulder seam.

⑤

Feeling through the toile to the jacket underneath, trace the front edge and rever with a chalk/cloth-marking pencil, from where the first panel starts to the shoulder point on the neckline. Mark in button and buttonhole positions.

⑥

Cut off excess fabric at the front, leaving around 1.5cm (½in), removing unnecessary pins.

⑦

Mark the seam line of the first panel, including the pocket. Trim away excess as before, pinning at shoulder, bust and waist (as shown) to hold panel in position.

⑧

Cut a new piece of cloth, big enough to make the second panel, with extra. Mark the horizontal bust line around halfway down.

DRAFTING TECHNIQUES
Rub-off pattern drafting

On the first cloth, clip into allowances at corners and along curves (as shown).

Place fabric onto jacket, matching bust line and ensuring that the grain remains at right angles. Pin in place.

Smooth fabric from bust to shoulder, pin up grainline. Pin and mark shoulder line.

Feeling through the cloth to the jacket underneath, mark off the seams.

Trim away excess back to 1.5cm (½in), and clip.

Cut a new rectangle of cloth, big enough for the side panel. Mark on bust line and waistline (distance as set in step 1).

⑮

Place fabric onto jacket, matching waistline, while ensuring that the grainline is at right angles. Smooth any excess fabric from waist towards underarm. Once flat, pin at underarm point.

⑯

Mark seams onto cloth as before. To help trace the underarm, trim away and clip into excess fabric, making it lay flatter. Trim back excess, leaving 1.5cm (½in).

⑰

Repeat for back panels, as front.

⑱

Prepare two pieces of fabric for the sleeve, approximately 76cm (30in) long by 38cm (15in). Mark a line down the centre of each panel, squaring another line across 20cm (8in) from the top. On the jacket, pin a line straight down from the shoulder seam. Pin a line level to the underarm point around the sleeve.

⑲

Place fabric on sleeve, matching central lines and underarm (bicep) line; pin down these lines. Wrap the fabric around the sleeve and pin at seams. Mark off seams and cuff.

⑳

Trace off cuff and seams up to armhole, marking notches at these points.

DRAFTING TECHNIQUES
Rub-off pattern drafting

21

smooth

CF

CF

22

CF

CF

CF

Smooth fabric up to sleevehead, pin at shoulder line (marking a notch there); then ease in excess evenly around the sleevehead (this is the ease the sleeve needs for a comfortable fit on the shoulder). Trim back to 1.5cm (½in) to remove unnecessary fabric; clip into allowances to help the sleevehead lay flat. Trace off sleevehead seam onto fabric.

Pin a line straight down from the underarm point on the sleeve; this will set the grain for the undersleeve. Take your second rectangle of fabric and pin in place to undersleeve, matching underarm line and grain. Trace off seams and cuff, trimming away excess to 1.5cm (½in).

23

CB

Cut a new piece of fabric for the collar, approximately 50cm (20in) wide and 21.5cm (8½in) deep. Draw a line 1.5cm (½in) up horizontally from the bottom edge; this amount is the allowance. Mark another line 10cm (4in) in from the left-hand edge; this is the CB and the grain of the collar section. Pin onto collar, matching CB and horizontal line with collar seam. Clip into allowance at 1–1.5cm (³⁄₈–½in) intervals, so that the fabric can follow the form of the collar.

24 smooth CB CF CF CF

Curve and pin fabric around neckline to front of collar. The horizontal collar line will not follow the seam from the shoulder line on the front. Pin where it lays flat. Trace off seam line and collar edge onto fabric. Trim off excess back to 1.5cm (½in) and clip into it again to help it lay flat. Unpin all sections and trace off onto pattern paper, pinning and/or weighting the pieces in place. Make sure that all lines are trued up and that right angles are correct. To aid this, mark a grainline on the pattern paper first, then mark any important lines (such as the waist or bust) that square across, and match draped garment sections to this. Curves should look good and flow without bumps. Make sure that connecting seams, such as the side seams, measure the same (this does not apply to seams that contain tolerance/ease or fullness). If not, true them up, referring back to the garment if needed.

1. Belted shirt dress.

(Photo credit: Simply Be)

DRAFTING TECHNIQUES

Rub-off pattern drafting

PATTERN DEVELOPMENT

CHAPTER 7:   VOLUME AND SUPPRESSION   106
- Volume   106
- Gathering   112
- Pleats   114

CHAPTER 8:   SLEEVES   116

CHAPTER 9:   COLLARS   124

CHAPTER 10:   WAISTBANDS AND CUFFS   130
- Waistbands   130
- Cuffs   134

CHAPTER 11:   OPENINGS AND FASTENINGS   136
- Openings   136
- Fastenings   146

CHAPTER 12:   HEMMING, FACINGS, AND LININGS   152
- Hemming   152
- Facings   154
- Linings   158

CHAPTER 13:   POCKETS   164

CHAPTER 7:
VOLUME AND SUPPRESSION

VOLUME

Even a basic close-fitting shape includes an amount of volume or 'tolerance', which, as the term suggests, allows tolerance (or ease) and movement within the garment to give a comfortable fit. This is even more relevant for over-garments, under which other clothes are worn.

When adding volume to a pattern piece, care must be taken where this is placed; extra flare can be given to the side seams, but if too much is given the garment becomes flat and wing-like. Volume is generally best spread evenly throughout the pattern piece in order to give a balanced and three-dimensional effect. Flare, too, must be added equally to front and back sections of a piece to keep the balance at the side seam; otherwise, the garment will twist or swing.

Once you understand the basic rules of adding fullness, you can play with controlling where the volume falls within a pattern piece. Whether you are creating a draped cowl or adding gather, volume is formed precisely at the points and direction that you slash and spread. This is especially relevant when asymmetrical flare is required.

The back is created in a similar manner: the back shoulder dart is closed, the bodice is divided and fullness is added. Ensure the side seam on the back bodice falls at the same angle as the front, or your garment will be skewed: to check, lay the back pattern over the front with shoulder neck points (SNP) touching and compare.

1. Roksanda Ilincic Astrae dress with added fullness at the waist gathered into a column skirt.
(Photo credit: Debenhams)

ADDING VOLUME TO BODICE WAIST

Remove and straighten the waist shaping on the side seams.

Pivot shoulder dart into waist dart.

Divide shoulder line into three equal sections and waist into four; split pattern as shown in diagram.

Spread sections as shown, opening equally to desired width.

Curve off hem and shoulder; redraw bust line as a curve. Repeat for back as front.

PATTERN DEVELOPMENT
Volume and suppression

BISHOP SLEEVES

Divide elbow line by six and square off a line vertically, dividing sleeve into equal sections.

Slash and spread as shown, opening sections at wrist to the desired width.

cut 1 pair

Add extra length as desired to sleeve at wrist (at least 2cm/¾in), to give a slight drop to sleeve. Curve off the sleevehead and redraw a new wrist line.

CLASSIC BISHOP SLEEVE

• To create a classic bishop sleeve (as shown in the diagram), add flare and length to the back half. This allows room for the elbow and creates a slight billow of volume at the back of the sleeve.

1. Star dress by Julien Macdonald with sheer bishop sleeve.

(Photo credit: Debenhams)

DECORATIVE TOLERANCE

• The excess fabric created at the crown can be further manipulated for decorative effect with the use of pleats, tucks or gathers to suppress the fullness.

LEG-OF-MUTTON SLEEVE

A leg-of-mutton sleeve is characterised by a full upper sleeve that narrows over the forearm and wrist. Varying amounts of fullness in the upper part of the sleeve combined with the addition of height to the crown can be used to give a sleeve with a subtle gathered and puffed cap or something altogether more ostentatious.

Take the basic sleeve block that has been slightly narrowed at the wrist line by 3–5cm (1¼–2in) (this manipulation can also be performed on the semi-fitted sleeve). Separate at the elbow and divide the upper portion of sleeve into four sections.

Slash and spread each upper section until the desired amount of fullness has been added.

Raise the crown to the desired amount and redraw the front and back seams, creating a smooth curve from underarm to wrist.

cut 1 pair

The finished pattern has seam allowance and annotation added.

PATTERN DEVELOPMENT
Volume and suppression

DRAPE AND COWL

Although unconstrained volume can be created by draping on the stand, the following examples show successful methods of creating flat pattern drape. In the diagrams on these pages, a cowl front is created in consecutive stages with progressively more volume added. In the Cowel Bodice diagrams, the bust dart is moved to the centre front; this adaptation is used to create a garment with a minimal amount of added volume in which the waist dart is retained (1 and 2). The waist dart can be used to create increasingly more volume (3 and 4). In these, the drape begins to fall from the SNP (shoulder neck point), while in the Drape From Mid-Shoulder diagrams, the CF is lowered and the shoulder shortened to create a drape that falls from mid-shoulder. In this example, the neckline has been straightened, which enables this style to be finished with an all-in-one facing (3). This method can also be used in combination with the back block to create a garment with a draped back.

CUTTING BIAS SHAPES

Cutting bias shapes on a fold is not recommended; the pattern piece should be mirrored for the most successful cut.

COWEL BODICE

Cut along chest line and close bust dart to transfer dart excess to CF.

Extend the centre front and connect to neckline.

1. Tunic with deep cowl falling from shoulder neck point.
(Photo credit: La Redoute)

2. Deep-cowl cardigan.
(Photo credit: Mint Velvet)

Closing the waist dart adds further depth to the cowl; again extend the CF line and connect to neckline.

Pivoting the upper section adds an increased amount of fullness into the cowl – note how the new CF line is now angled.

DRAPE FROM MID-SHOULDER

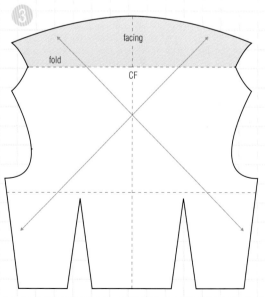

Mark and slash red lines as shown.

Extend CF line and pivot released sections until uppermost segment runs at a 90-degree angle to CF.

The finished pattern piece with an all-in-one facing.

PATTERN DEVELOPMENT

Volume and suppression

GATHERING

Gathers are a form of constrained fullness or suppression. They are produced by drawing up a set measurement of fabric to fit a smaller area. Gathers can be ordered and spread evenly, or bunched and irregular. The type of fabric used will vary the effect: soft materials will drape; crisp fabrics will hold form and billow.

When creating gathered patterns, a ratio needs to be specified (for example, 2:1) for the amount that the gathered section needs to be drawn up to fit the smaller section. This simplifies the pattern for the machinist.

Gathers can utilise the dart shaping already present in a basic block, or extra fullness can be added by slashing and spreading the pattern in the direction of the required volume.

GATHERS

There are a number of ways to form gathers, each of which will produce a different effect.

- **Ruffles** are gathered strips of fabric that are inserted into seams, which can be single- or multilayered.

- **Shirring** is a form of gathering, and can be created by using elasticated or 'shirring' thread only on the bobbin and a normal top thread. The tensioned stretch in the bobbin thread will contract and gather the sewn stitch line.

- **Smocking** is another type of gathering, albeit more complicated and ornamental. Points of fabric are sewn together in alternate rows, giving a honeycomb effect.

1. Lace skater dress with Peter Pan collar.
(Photo credit: Missguided.co.uk)

2. Luxury ruche dress with asymmetrical gathered panels.
(Photo credit: Freemans)

SEWING GATHERS

With a large stitch length, sew two lines, one just in from the stitch line on the seam allowance, and a second 6mm (¼in) in. Do not back-tack, and leave thread ends long. By pulling the thread ends of the bobbin thread, gather the seam allowance to the ratio set on the pattern, making sure that gathers are spread evenly – using two stitch lines helps with this. Pin the gathered piece onto the smaller piece and, with a normal stitch length, sew the seam. Overlock the raw edges, and press the seam allowances in the direction away from the gathers. Gathered areas can be pressed by opening up the area flat and pressing as far into the gather as possible. Do not press over the gathers, as they will flatten, spoiling the effect.

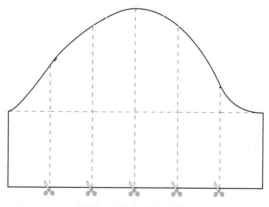

slash and spread to desired amount

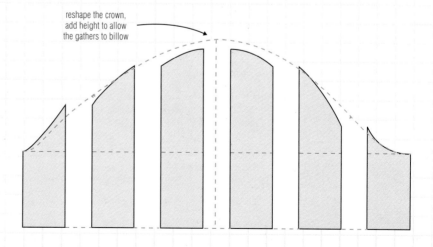

reshape the crown,
add height to allow
the gathers to billow

PATTERN DEVELOPMENT
Volume and suppression

PLEATS

Pleats are pressed folds that suppress volume through part or all of a garment section. They can be used singularly or repeated; allowed to open and fall freely, or stitched down and released at a specific point. Such a pleat is used at the back of a jacket lining to give an extra amount of volume across the shoulders for a comfortable fit.

Pleats can give flare and 'swing' to a garment, and enable a large amount of volume to be present while still having a fitted silhouette. Pleating can utilise a lot of fabric: a typical pleat ratio is 3:1. Fold lines must be marked accurately, and match points notched.

Certain fabrics pleat more easily than others; materials with a polyester content can be permanently heat-set, whereas other synthetics such as acrylic do not have good pleat retention.

It is advisable to hem any areas before pleating, as hemming afterwards will spoil the pleating. Companies specialising in pleating are able to produce an amazing variety of intricate pleat designs, which appear more like paper origami than fabric.

GRAIN PLACEMENT

The grain plays an important part in pleats. Vertical pleats, such as those on a trouser front, should follow the straight grain; otherwise the pleat is liable to twist.

TYPES OF PLEATS

Knife pleats: these lay in one direction only.

fold · placement line · fold · placement line · fold · placement line · fold · placement line

1. Tailored linen dress with scalloped neckline and inverted-box-pleat skirt.

(Photo credit: ASOS)

Box pleats/inverted box pleats: These lay in two opposite directions. Box pleats have pleats that turn away from one another, while inverted box pleats face one another.

MIRRORING A PLEAT

This ensures that the pleat excess maintains the same profile as the seam allowance after construction. Add pleat width to pattern, then fold paper, placing pleat excess in desired direction. Trace the yoke profile to the folded pleat. Open out the pattern piece, noting the extended profile of the pleat.

PATTERN DEVELOPMENT
Volume and suppression

CHAPTER 8:
SLEEVES

In this chapter, a range of sleeve techniques is provided to add variety to your designs. A well-set-in sleeve will frame a garment, and care and attention should be shown at the construction phase to ensure consistency. Refer to the diagram on p. 44 for a reminder as to the correct method of construction.

After pattern manipulation is complete, measure the front and back armhole and crown, making a note of these figures on your patterns. You will note that the crown measurement is greater than that of the combined armhole; this is to be expected, as this tolerance (ease) is an allowance for the fullness of the upper arm and shoulder. Depending on fabric choice, it may be necessary to reduce this tolerance – refer to the fitting and alteration technique on p. 87 to complete this.

1. Chiffon blouse with oversized kimono-style inset sleeves.
(Photo credit: ASOS)

2. Button-front shirt with bishop-style sleeve gathered at the wrist.
(Photo credit: Lipsy)

DECORATIVE ELBOW DART

The elbow dart can be further manipulated for decorative effect. Consider tucks, pleats or a series of pin tucks to suppress this fullness.

SEMI-FITTED SLEEVE

This sleeve could be considered a block in its own right; it may be worth copying onto card to save time manipulating the basic sleeve block if used frequently. As its name suggests, the semi-fitted sleeve gives a closer fit at the wrist, as well as creating a dart at the elbow.

BASIC SLEEVE

3cm (1¼in)   3cm (1¼in)

Measure in from the wrist line 3cm (1¼in) and connect this point to the underarm point.

overlap 4cm (1½in)

Cut along the centre line of the sleeve up to the elbow line and again from the elbow line to the centre to release the back section of the sleeve below the elbow. Pivot this section to create an overlap of approximately 4cm (1½in) at the wrist line, thus creating a new dart at the elbow.

SEMI-FITTED SLEEVE cut 1 pair

Make a new copy of your sleeve, reducing the elbow dart by half its length. Add seam allowances and pattern annotation.

PATTERN DEVELOPMENT
Sleeves

RAGLAN SLEEVES

Often associated with sportswear, providing a comfortable fit and offering a free range of movement, this adaptation is particularly suitable for activewear garments and knitwear patterning. This style combines the shoulder section of the front and back bodice patterns with the sleeve. In its simplest form, a diagonal seam runs from the neckline to the underarm: a baseball shirt is a good example of this.

A raglan sleeve can be drafted in one piece, with a dart at the sleevehead to provide suppression at the shoulder, or it can be converted into a two-piece sleeve by separating the sleeve on the centre line and adding seam allowances. While the drafting procedure may seem a little tricky to the beginner, it is easier to construct than a set-in sleeve.

The first stage is to temporarily move the back shoulder dart; the front bust dart will also need to be moved for the duration of this drafting process. Next, trace around the basic sleeve block and lower the crown to remove excess tolerance (ease) from the sleevehead (see p. 87).

Lay the front and back bodice blocks onto the traced sleeve, matching balance points but leaving a 7mm (5/16in) gap between the SNP and centre of the sleeve. Create a dart at the sleevehead of approximately 5cm (2in) to give a smooth run at the shoulder. Draw in your required seam lines, ensuring they blend into the bodice and sleeve at the balance points.

Trace off new pieces, closing the temporary back shoulder dart and bust dart if necessary, and add seam allowances and pattern annotation.

Repeat step 2 for the raglan back and front, tracing off new pieces, closing the temporary back shoulder dart and bust dart if necessary, and add seam allowances and pattern annotation.

CAPES

Cape patterns can be generated from your basic blocks in much the same way as the flat collars described on p. 125. Before completing the cape exercises, the bodice and sleeve blocks can be adapted to centralise the shoulder line.

GENERATING A CAPE BLOCK

ignore dart

08

line blocks SNP to SNP

redraw back armhole to match front

move shoulder line forwards 1cm (³⁄₈in)

CF

bust

move shoulder notch forwards 1cm (³⁄₈in)

Sleeve

Lay front and back blocks together with SNP touching, and redraw the back shoulder line 1cm (³⁄₈in) forwards. Redraw the back armhole to create a smooth run with front armhole and ignore the back shoulder dart.

Although the sleeve block is not necessary for the cape drafting procedures, this adaptation can also be used in conjunction with the raglan drafting method described above; to this end, the shoulder notch is moved forwards 1cm (³⁄₈in) to match the newly situated shoulder line.

| PATTERN DEVELOPMENT |
| Sleeves |

CAPE WITH FULL-FLUTED HEM

To create a cape of any length with a full-fluted hem:

Lay patterns together with front and back SNP touching and mark the desired length at CB. Extend shoulder line measurement using CB measurement plus 6cm (2½in) (a) and mark CF at CB measurement plus 2.5cm (1in) (b). Connect these points to create the outer (hem) edge of your cape, as shown in diagram. The cape can be cut in one or a seam can be created at the shoulder line, aligning grain to CB and CF.

1. Sequin cape with full-flared hem.

(Photo credit: Internacionale)

2. Canvas and merino cape with reduced hem.

(Photo credit: Land's End)

CAPE WITH LESS FLARE IN HEM

To create a cape of any length with less flare in the hem:

Align blocks with shoulder points touching and pivot SNP until blocks are positioned at a 90-degree angle to each other. Again, mark CB length and determine shoulder seam and CF length using the measurements described above. Trace the front and back draft, ensuring that side seam measurements match (a).

Fullness can be further constrained at the side seam (this additional shaping is shown in grey on the diagram) (b).

ALL-IN-ONE CAP SLEEVE

To create a short sleeve cut in one with the main body of the garment:

Raise the shoulder line by 1cm (⅜in) (a). Extend the shoulder line and connect to the bodice side seams, marking the end of the sleeve opening with a notch (b).

raise shoulder 1cm (⅜in)

mark end of sleeve
opening with a notch

bust

TWO-PIECE SLEEVE

A two-piece sleeve follows the natural curve of the arm and can be used to great effect on fitted or tailored garments. This sleeve can be cut using the basic sleeve block or the semi-fitted sleeve.

Omit stage 1 if your starting point is the basic sleeve block.

SEMI-FITTED
SLEEVE

close
dart

SEMI-FITTED
SLEEVE

wrist

Fold out the elbow dart and straighten the wrist.

2.5cm (1in) 2.5cm (1in)

8cm (3¼in)

16cm (6¼in)

8cm (3¼in)

16cm (6¼in)

1cm (⅜in) 1cm (⅜in)

spread 2cm (¾in)

overlap 2cm (¾in)

Fold sleeve so that the underarm seams touch the centre line, and pin or tape into position. Measure 2.5cm (1in) in from fold at the bicep level and 1cm (⅜in) at wrist. Connect these two points with a straight line to create the new seams for your two-piece sleeve. Now mark notches either side of the elbow, approximately 8cm (3¼in) on the back sleeve and 16cm (6¼in) on the front.

Cut through the elbow line, pivoting the released section downwards by 2cm (¾in); tape or pin into place. Notice how the back seam is now longer and the front seam is shorter: this discrepancy will be eased and stretched during construction.

Cut up the seam lines created in step 3 to separate your sleeve into two pieces, opening out the fold created in step 2, to create a top sleeve and the undersleeve.

Add pattern annotation and seam allowances and mark the areas to be stretched or eased (tolerance).

TOP SLEEVE cut 1 pair

ease stretch

UNDER-SLEEVE cut 1 pair

stretch ease

PATTERN DEVELOPMENT

Sleeves

CHAPTER 9: COLLARS

Before drafting any of the following collars, lower or adjust the neckline as the individual design dictates. Using the tape measure on its side, measure the neckline, making a note of the complete and individual front and back neckline measurements.

It should be noted, as a general principle, that the length of the outer edge of a collar dictates its resting position in a finished garment. A reduction in length encourages the collar to sit higher on the shoulder line, creating a roll at the neckline. To see this principle in action, pin small darts or make slashes regularly around the leaf edge of a sample collar to observe the effects. You will notice that as the roll of a collar increases, the width of the collar may also need to be extended to accommodate this.

There are three basic types of collar: stand-up, shirt and flat.

If a top collar and undercollar are required, add 2.5–5cm (1–2in) to the neck and outer edge of the top collar. This addition will ensure the top collar rolls under out of sight, so the bagged-out edge does not show upon wear.

LOWERING NECKLINES

Lowering the neckline by approximately 1cm (³/₈in) at the centre front to nothing at the shoulder neck point (SNP) can improve the fit of most types of collar and will also avoid the collar feeling restrictive upon wear.

CUTTING COLLARS

Collars can be cut on a fold, or the draft can be mirrored and cut on a single layer. Tracing and cutting your finished collar draft onto a folded piece of paper will speed up the mirroring process.

1. Top with Peter Pan collar.
(Photo credit: Fever)

FLAT COLLARS

An important point to remember when drafting flat collars is that the greater
the overlap at the shoulders, the more the leaf edge of a flat collar will be reduced.
When drafting a flat collar for a pattern of your own design that has a bust dart
situated at the shoulder or neckline, temporarily move or close this dart while
you draft the collar. (This principle does not apply to the back shoulder dart.)

PETER PAN COLLAR

A Peter Pan collar is a rounded, flat collar without a stand, although this
drafting method can be used to great effect with any shaped collar of your
choice. The example below will give a collar with very little roll at the neckline:
Increase the overlap at the shoulder to create a collar with more roll.

overlap 2cm
(¾in)

CF

80

Lower the neckline first if necessary. Lay the front and back pattern pieces together
with the shoulder neck points touching and the shoulder points overlapping by
approximately 2cm (¾in). Draw the desired collar shape, ensuring you mark notches
at the shoulder seams.

UNDER-
COLLAR
cut 1 x self
cut 1 x fuse

CB

Trace a copy of your collar, adding
seam allowances and annotation
in the usual manner. Remember the
undercollar will also require interlining
or fusing, so ensure you add this
instruction to the pattern piece.

TOP COLLAR
cut 1 x self

CB

Make another copy of your collar.
Before adding seam allowances, add
an extra 3mm (⅛in) to its leaf and neck
edges, as shown in the diagram, to
ensure that your top collar will roll
neatly and will not expose any of
the bagged-out seam.

PATTERN DEVELOPMENT
Collars

ETON COLLAR

An Eton collar is very similar to a Peter Pan collar; it is a flat collar with no stand but has a flat leaf edge and sits a little higher and wider on the neckline. The example below will give a collar with a partial roll at the neckline: increase the overlap at the shoulder as your design dictates.

overlap 4cm
(1½in)

UNDER-
COLLAR
cut 1 x self
cut 1 x fuse

CB

TOP COLLAR
cut 1 x self

CB

Lower the neckline first if necessary. Lay the front and back pattern pieces together with the shoulder neck points touching and the shoulder points overlapping by approximately 4cm (1½in). Draw the desired collar shape, ensuring you mark notches at the shoulder seams.

Follow Peter Pan instructions from step 2 (see p. 125).

MANDARIN COLLAR

A Mandarin collar is simple band collar that has been shaped at the neck edge to follow the profile of the neck. The following example exhibits the minimum of shaping; a deeper collar may require more. Adjust as your design dictates.

Draft a rectangle using the combined front and back measurements in length and approximately 3.5cm (1⅜in) in height. Mark the shoulder notch position using half the back measurement as a guide. Mark a dashed line vertically through the collar at the shoulder notch.

Slash the collar draft along the dashed line and pivot the upper edge, overlapping pieces by 4mm (³⁄₁₆in). Shape the centre front of the collar if required.

Trace two copies of your manipulated pattern, smoothing the overlapping lines to create smooth continuous curves. Add seam allowances and pattern annotation, remembering to add a turning allowance to the top collar.

1. Dress with Eton collar. (Photo credit: ASOS)

PATTERN DEVELOPMENT
Collars

SHIRT COLLARS

TWO-PIECE SHIRT COLLAR

This traditional two-piece collar is drafted with the Mandarin collar in the previous example as a basis. Lower the neckline 6mm (¼ in) at centre front.

Follow stage 1 of the Mandarin collar draft; this will become the stand for your two-piece collar. At a 90-degree angle from the CF add a button-stand extension if required.

Draft the collar fall, squaring from the CB and using the upper edge of the Mandarin collar as a guide.

Divide the collar into thirds.

spread 3mm (⅛in)

Spread each collar section 3mm (⅛in).

Trace two copies of your manipulated pattern. Add seam allowances and pattern annotation, remembering to add a bagging-out allowance to the top collar.

TOP COLLAR
cut 1 x self

UNDER-COLLAR
cut 1 x self
+ 1 x fuse

COLLAR STAND
cut 1 pair self
+ 1 x fuse

1. Oversize blouse with two-piece shirt collar.

(Photo credit: Fashion Union)

REVER COLLAR

Follow this drafting method for high rever styles that break above the bust line. For a rever on a low neckline, ensure that excess tolerance (ease) is removed from the neckline as shown on p. 59.

Add a button stand to the bodice draft and draft the rever shape. Connect base of rever to shoulder neck point with a straight dashed line and label the break point.

Fold paper along the break line and trace through the rever shape.

Mark the facing position and trace off a copy, adding a turning allowance to the lead edge of the facing.

2. Dress with contrast rever.

(Photo credit: Dunnes)

PATTERN DEVELOPMENT

Collars

CHAPTER 10:
WAISTBANDS AND CUFFS

WAISTBANDS

Waistbands are used to finish and support the waist of a garment. Select from the following techniques, depending on the desired placement in relation to the waistline.

STRAIGHT WAISTBAND ON THE WAIST

A straight waistband is the simplest of waistbands; it can be used successfully if set on the waistline and drafted in widths between 2.5 and 8cm (1–3¼ in). This drafting method is also suitable for use as a channel for an elastic or a ribbed waistband or a band cuff.

The instructions below apply to both a wide waistband (as shown in top diagram right and upper diagram below) or to a narrow waistband (as shown in bottom diagram right and lower diagram below). Measure the waistline of your pattern, remembering to subtract the total dart excess. Draft a rectangle to this measurement × double the width of the finished waistband. (If fabric economy is a consideration, draft pattern to single waistband width and cut 1 × lining, 1 × self.) Mark CB, CF and side seam with notches. Mark the fold line with a dashed line. If required, add an under-wrap and mark button and buttonhole position. Add seam allowances and pattern annotation.

WIDE WAISTBAND WITH SIDE-SEAM OPENING

CB		CF	
fold			
cut 1 × self + fuse			

NARROW WAISTBAND WITH CENTRE-BACK OPENING

CB	fold	CF	CB
cut 1 × self + fuse			

SHAPED WAISTBAND BELOW THE WAIST

Waistbands set below the waistline require shaping to fit the contours of the body and should be cut singly and fused.

1

Trim required amount from waistline of skirt pattern and record this lowered waist measurement. Using the general (or personal) waist measurement, make a straight waistband as described opposite.

2

Slash at CB, CF and side seam, spreading the lower edge until it is the same length as the newly created low waistline measurement recorded in stage 1.

3

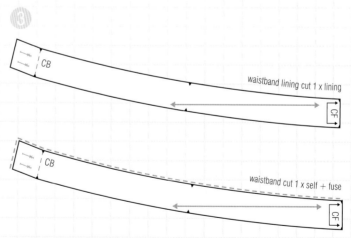

Smooth off shaped waistband and add button stand if required. Add seam allowances and pattern annotation.

PATTERN DEVELOPMENT
Waistbands and cuffs

SHAPED WAISTBAND ABOVE THE WAIST

Waistbands set above the waistline require shaping to fit the body. Shaped waistbands need to be cut singly and fused.

waistline

Trace shaped bodice block and draw in desired waistband. Cut out waistband and close darts.

Trace around pattern and create a continuous line, smoothing closed dart legs. Draft button-wrap if required, then add seam allowance and pattern annotation.

FRONT WAISTBAND
cut 1 x self + fuse

FRONT WAISTBAND
cut 1 x self + fuse

Trace another copy, adding 3mm (⅛in) for turning. Further shaping may be required at side seams; ensure that you are aware of the measurement of both skirt and block waistlines to assess the required reduction. Side seams can be joined and blended for a CB or CF opening.

waistline

LOW-RISE WAISTBAND

Only very narrow straight waistbands should be drafted using this method: maximum width 2.5cm (1in). For deeper waistbands, use the shaped waistband method described on p. 131. You may also want to consider removing 6mm (¼in) from the front and back waistline side seams, running smoothly to the hip for an improved fit. Mark lowered waistline on skirt pattern 5–6cm (2–2½in) below waistline and create a straight waistband to fit.

ALTERNATIVE WAIST FINISHES

Waistbands can also be finished with a waistband facing or bias binding.

1. Paper-bag waistline skirt with contrast waistband.
(Photo credit: Very)

2. Skirt with below-the-waist shaped waistband.
(Photo credit: Littlewoods)

CUFFS

Before cuffs are added, the sleeve guard or relevant opening must be completed. Cuffs can be attached before or after the sleeve is sewn into the armhole, depending on the type of sleeve and the desired construction process. However, remember that most cuff types can only be attached after the underarm seam has been sewn.

SHIRT CUFF

Plan cuff to desired measurements; if required, add an over- and/or underlap. Mark the extension with a notch if applicable.

1. Holly Willoughby large-collar blouse.

(Photo credit: Very)

SHAPED CUFF

Due to its curved profile, a shaped cuff cannot be cut on the fold. To this end, plan cuff to desired measurements, adding an over- or underlap if required. Trace another copy, add a turning allowance to the outer edges, and label it 'top cuff'.

Add interfacing to provide stability and sew the pieces together. Prepare the cuff for bagging out by snipping the curve, cutting out triangles of fabric to remove bulk and grading the seam allowances to reduce excess.

ATTACHING A BAGGED-OUT SECTION

The following construction method describes the method of construction for a lapped cuff with an opening, but the technique is much the same to attach any bagged-out shape, such as a collar or waistband.

Plan cuff to desired measurements; if required, add an over- and/or underlap. Mark the extension with a notch if applicable.

Press SA on one long side of cuff piece to WS.

Fold the cuff in half, RS together, and sew both short sides. Stop stitching at SA fold. Mitre corners to reduce bulk. Bag out cuff and press.

Place the unpressed cuff edge to the inside of the sleeve hem, lining up the notch with the opening edge. RS of the cuff fabric should be facing the WS of the sleeve fabric. Sew cuff to sleeve, stopping stitching at extension notch and ensuring stitching does not catch the folded SA.

Turn cuff to the RS and press the seam down inside the cuff. Trim any areas of excess fabric that may cause unnecessary bulk. Close the cuff edge with an edge-stitch through all layers. All raw seam edges will be enclosed in the cuff. Topstitch the cuff if desired.

PATTERN DEVELOPMENT
Waistbands and cuffs

CHAPTER 11: OPENINGS AND FASTENINGS

OPENINGS

Areas of the garment such as the neckline or the cuff may require additional openings to allow for the head or hand to pass through. For dresses, skirts and trousers, this opening commonly goes to the hip line. If an opening in an existing seam is not possible or desired, an opening can be created with a placket. A placket is typically a doubled fabric section that supports button fastenings, and is usually found on the CF and cuff of a shirt. When considering openings, you must also decide the methods by which they, in turn, are closed. The variety of closures or fastenings is covered in the next section.

ALL-IN-ONE BUTTON STAND

An all-in-one button stand can be used on reversible fabrics. As you can see from the construction diagram, this button stand is created in one piece so the wrong side of the fabric is folded back, and on view (as part of the outer). The right-hand side (RHS) and left-hand side (LHS) of this opening are drafted in the same manner, but, as you will see from the diagram, they are not sewn in the same way.

DRAFTING AN ALL-IN-ONE BUTTON STAND

RHS: from the centre front draw a dashed line 1 x the width of the button. Mark this line as 'fold' (1).

RHS: from the fold line, draw another line at 2 x the width of the button (2).

LHS: repeat steps 1 and 2 as for RHS (3).

Mark button and buttonhole positions (4).

Add seam allowances and pattern annotation, noting areas to fuse (5).

SEPARATE BUTTON STAND

This type of button stand is suitable for fabrics that cannot be turned to show the wrong side of the fabric due to obvious differences between the different sides of the fabric. This type of button stand would also be used on a garment style with a yoke seam, which would otherwise bisect the button stand.

DRAFTING A SEPARATE BUTTON STAND

RHS: from the centre front, draw a dashed line 1 x the width of the button and mark this line as 'fold' (1).

LHS: from the centre front, draw a dashed line 1 x the width of the button and mark this line as 'fold' (2).

LHS: from the fold line, draw another at 2 x the width of the button (3).

Mark button and buttonhole positions (4).

Add seam allowances and pattern annotation, noting areas to fuse (5).

MARKING BUTTONHOLES

Buttons should be selected that are appropriate for the purpose, and of a suitable size for the location and thickness of fabric. Buttons can be either sew-through or with a shank; sew-through buttons tend to be better for thinner fabrics, whereas the shank allows for thicker materials.

SHIRT SLEEVE PLACKET (SLEEVE GUARD)

A sleeve placket allows for an opening at the cuff of a shirt. There are many variations of placket; common to all of them is the creation of an overlap (the placket), which is the more visible part, and the underlap, which is hidden.

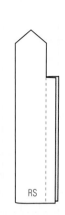

To draft the placket, decide the length needed for the slit opening (around 11cm/4¼in). Draw a rectangle this height plus around 3cm (1¼in) for the top of the placket; the width should be twice the desired finished width of the placket (finished width say, 2cm/¾in). Add 1.2cm (½in) seam allowances to the bottom and top edges, and 6mm (¼in) to each side.

Fold the placket in half, right sides facing, and pin. Mark the desired shape of the top of the placket (i.e. rounded, pointed, squared) and stitch this line from the folded edge to the notch at the side. Trim back the seam allowance to 6mm (¼in) and clip at the notch to release seam allowances; if the placket has an angled top then mitre off to the point. NB: from here, this example refers to a placket with a pointed end.

Turn out the placket, pull out the seam allowance at the notch point and press the seam flat.

TIP

It may be necessary to fuse the placket and underlap; this must be decided before you start construction.

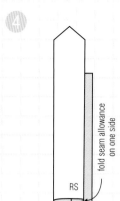

Fold and press the seam allowance to the wrong side of the placket.

UNDERLAP

The underlap is the length of the slit plus seam allowances of 1.5cm (½in) at each end. The width should be 3cm (1¼in), which includes 6mm (¼in) seam allowance, giving a finished binding of 1cm (⅜in).

On the sleeve, reinforce the opening by staystitching 6mm (¼in) away from the marked slit all around. Cut up the slit to within 1cm (⅜in) of the top and then clip into the corners. At this point, decide the front and back edges of the opening; this will determine which side the placket is sewn upon. Align the RS of the unfolded seam allowance of the underlap to the WS back edge of the slit, and stitch. Press the seam allowances into the underlap, then fold the underlap towards the RS, encasing the raw edges. Pin the folded edge over to cover the first seam and edge-stitch through all the layers, stopping at the top corner.

Fold the triangular section at the top of the slit and pin it to the underlap. Stitch together across the bottom of the triangle.

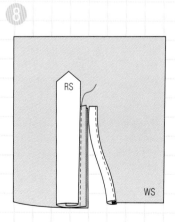

Align the RS of the unfolded placket edge to the WS of the front slit edge, pin and stitch.

Press the seam allowances into the placket, trimming to reduce bulk if necessary. Turn the placket through to the RS, aligning the folded edge of the placket to the first stitch line. Pin or tack to keep in place.

Edge-stitch through all the layers, from the cuff continuing up the side of the folded placket edge, pivoting around the point at the top of the placket, and finishing by sewing across the top of the slit (to reinforce), as shown.

1. Pin-tuck dress.

(Photo credit: Internacionale)

BOUND PLACKET

This method may be done with a binding attachment on your sewing machine.
It is used mainly for shirts, where the cuffs are cuff-linked together,
and for lightweight or sheer fabrics, as it gives a clean, 'unworked' look that is
extremely durable. As the edges overlap, it can be used with any lapped cuff.

Cut a self-bias binding 3cm (1¼in) wide
and twice the length of the marked slit.
Press one side 6mm (¼in) under to the
WS and mark a 6mm (¼in) seam along
the other side.

Reinforce the placket by staystitching
from the edge to the point, pivoting and
stitching back to the edge. Slash to
the point.

Open out the slit and pin the binding
to the sleeve, right sides facing, with
the unfolded edge aligned as shown.
Stitch, and press seam allowances
towards the binding.

TIP

For more accuracy, drop down to
a lower stitch length when stitching
up to corners.

Fold the binding over to the WS,
encasing the raw edges. Line up the
folded edge with the stitching line,
pin in place and edge-stitch.

The finished binding.

PATTERN DEVELOPMENT
Openings and fastenings

ONE-PIECE PLACKET BAND

This type of placket is suitable for either neck or sleeve openings.

cut-off section

Draw a rectangle the length of the slit opening plus at least 2.5cm (1in) (this is for the overlap that reinforces the placket) and seam allowances (6mm /¼in). The width should be five times the required finished width of placket (determined by button size and design specifications) plus seam allowances (for the top edge, use the seam allowance used on the neckline on the body of the garment).

On the middle section of the placket, mark seam allowances for the opening.

The placket is drafted with one side longer than the other; this creates the overlap that in womenswear is on the right-hand side and in menswear on the left. The underlap side should be made 1.5cm (⅝in) shorter so that its raw edge is enclosed by the overlap. On the underlap side, square off a line 1.5cm (⅝in) up from the bottom to below the overlap seam and square down.

cut 1 x pair + fuse

cut-off section

Remove this rectangle from the main section.

Apply interfacing (if necessary) to the wrong sides of the placket. Fold and press in seam allowances on the sides, and pin or tack at the bottom edge of the front band if necessary.

Pin the RS of the placket to the WS of the garment, aligning markings. Stitch along seam lines, pivoting at the corners.

Snip into the corners and trim seam allowances if needed. Turn the placket through to the RS of the garment. Press the long seams inwards towards the placket and press the triangular end down. Fold and press the shorter placket side along the fold line, positioning the edge over the original seam line, and pin. Edge-stitch along the folded edge.

Fold and press the other (longer) side of the placket along the fold line, positioning the edge over the original seam line, and pin in place. Edge-stitch along the folded edge, from top to bottom, and, pivoting on corners, carry on stitching as shown so that both placket sides are stitched together and all raw edges are enclosed.

PATTERN DEVELOPMENT

Openings and fastenings

FASTENINGS

Fastenings are more than just a functional detail on a garment, allowing garment openings to be securely closed. They can be used to enhance design and to attract focus to an area of the garment, as well as contrast visual styles.

ZIPS

Zips are one of the most commonly used forms of garment fastening; they are strong and can be applied in many ways. Their most typical use is to join two parts, or sides, of a garment, but they can also enable sections of a garment to be detachable, allowing multifunctional use. Because of the gradual method of opening/closing, zips can both restrict and provide fullness to an area of a garment, which can be used to great effect.

Zips can be included for visual purposes, and made to an array of designs, varying in length, the size and type of teeth (metal, plastic, coil), type and size of tape (nylon, cotton, coated) and type of zip pull (plastic, metal, rubber, leather). Zips can have two sliders, which enable them to open from either end. There are five main types of zip:

- **Plain:** A versatile zip used for trouser flies and pocket openings, these are usually topstitched into position, leaving a visible line of stitching.

- **Invisible:** This is the least conspicuous of the zips, giving the impression that it is just a seam. As the slider mechanism, tape and teeth are hidden on the inside of the garment, only the pull is seen.

- **Separating:** This opens up completely and splits into two halves, and is ideal for openings on jackets, outerwear and tops. It can be used for design purposes on garments where a full opening is not essential but part of the look of the piece.

- **Invisible separating:** Sometimes known as bodice zips, these also open up completely but give the look of an invisible zip, which is inconspicuous when fastened.

- **Lightweight invisible:** This is a lighter-weight, gauzy tape that is more suitable for softer, thinner fabrics, where a conventional zip would shadow through or distort the garment.

top tape extension

top stop

slider

pull tab

teeth or coil

bottom stop

bottom tape extension

OTHER TYPES OF FASTENINGS

The chosen method of closure depends on many factors, such as the type and look of garment, fabric weight and the position of the fastening. The following are various common fastenings and their usage.

- **Buttons:** Please refer to the previous section. (1)

- **Snaps:** Also known as press studs and poppers, snaps have two interlocking parts, which click (or snap) together, and come apart when pulled. They can be either sewn on or riveted (for more heavy-duty garments), and can be used in conjunction with other fasteners such as a zip. (2)

- **Hooks and eyes:** These sewn-on fastenings are formed of bent wire. They are composed of two parts: a hook, and a flat eyelet into which the hook fits when fastened. They are available in a range of sizes and finishes, including thread-covered (which can also be done by hand). Hooks and eyes are ideal for fabrics with a long pile, such as fur, which would trap within any other fastenings. They can be used as a fastening on their own (in a series of hooks and eyes) or with others, such as to ensure secure closure at the top of a zip. (3)

VISIBLE ZIP

The visible zip method needs a plain zip, and can be used for decorative effect. This type of zip can be inserted into a section of a garment without the need for a seam. This method can be adapted to create a letterbox-style visible zip, suitable for pocket openings. The facing used to create the opening for the zip can be attached to a lining or the edge finished off in another method, such as binding or overlocking.

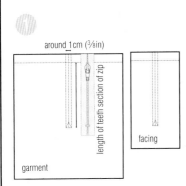

Mark the location and length of the opening on the pattern. The opening should be the length of the teeth of the zip.

With right sides together, align garment body with facing at the opening. Pin and stitch around the opening, as shown, pivoting on corners. Cut through the centre of the opening from the seam allowance to the point of the triangular section, and clip diagonal lines into corners.

Turn through facing to wrong side of garment.

Press.

Place zip behind facing, aligning teeth in the centre of the opening, and pin.

Edge-stitch zip into position.

SEMI-CONCEALED ZIP

This method needs a plain zip, and can be used for both closed and open-ended zip insertions.

RS garment

Draft seam allowances of 1cm (³⁄₈in) on both seam edges.

WS garment

Place the zip so that the top stopper aligns just below the stitch line, as shown. Mark the bottom of the lower metal stopper with a pin.

WS garment

Stitch the seam, right sides together, up to this point.

WS garment

Press seam allowances open.

RS garment

Place the zip behind the opening, centring the zip on the seam, and pin into position.

RS garment

With a zipper foot, topstitch around the opening at approximately 4–6mm (³⁄₁₆–¼in) out.

PATTERN DEVELOPMENT
Openings and fastenings

CONCEALED ZIP

This method uses a plain zip. It is a suitable opening for skirts and trousers.

Draft seam allowances of 1cm (⅜in) on both seam edges.

Place the zip so that the top stopper aligns just below the stitch line, as shown. Mark with a pin the bottom of the lower metal stopper.

Stitch the seam, right sides together, up to this point.

Press seam allowances open.

On the left-hand side, fold out seam allowance.

Fold SA along opening, 3–4mm (⅛–³⁄₁₆in) from seam, continuing for 5cm (2in) below end of zip. Place zip below, aligning fold 2mm (¹⁄₁₆in) away from teeth, and pin.

Open up zip, and edge-stitch using the zipper foot for the length of the zip. To stitch past the zip slider: with the needle down, lift the foot and pull the slider past, then continue sewing.

Pin the other side of the zip to the right-hand side.

Topstitch into position with the zipper foot, following the edge of the zip teeth, about 2mm (¹⁄₁₆in) out. Sewing towards the edge helps prevent a tuck forming at the bottom of the zip.

INVISIBLE ZIP

This method is probably the most commonly used zip type for dresses, skirts and some tops. Buy invisible zips slightly longer (1.5cm/½in) than the length required, as part of the length of the zip is used when constructing.

Draft 1.5cm (½in) seam allowances on both seam edges.

At the bottom of the zip, pin a point 1.5cm (½in) above the bottom stop, align the zip as shown to the seam and pin this point on the seam.

Stitch the seam up to this point.

Press seam allowances open.

Fold out seam allowances on one side.

Align and pin the zip to seam allowances. Open up the zip and, using an invisible zipper foot, stitch the zip to the seam allowance, opening out the zip teeth as you go to ensure the zip is stitched closely. Stitch down the zip to as far as the foot will allow.

Repeat for the other side.

Push the zip pull through (there will be a small gap between the two sides at the bottom of the zip) and close the zip. Press.

PATTERN DEVELOPMENT
Openings and fastenings

CHAPTER 12: FINISHINGS, LININGS AND FACINGS

HEMMING

Hems can be finished in a wide variety of ways; consider binding, perhaps in a lighter-weight fabric such as georgette. Alternatively, a raw or overlocked edge may be suitable for your specific design. A market-appropriate hem finish will give your garment a professional look. The most common hem finishes are listed below.

TURN AND OVERLOCK HEM

This is often the cheapest and quickest hem to turn, and is suitable for a wide variety of fabrics. Hem turn allowance can be adjusted as individual design dictates.

fold

Overlock edge.

Fold hem allowance and stitch.

DOUBLE-TURN HEM

This is a self-neatening hem suitable for non-bulky fabrics, which can be sewn in conjunction with a topstitched or handstitched finish. Hem turn allowance can be adjusted as the individual design dictates.

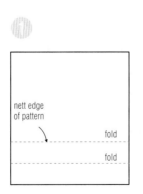

nett edge of pattern

fold

fold

Fold first turn allowance into position.

topstitch

Fold second turn allowance and topstitch: the raw edge is concealed in the double-turned fabric.

MACHINE-ROLLED HEM

A machine-rolled hem is a narrow, double-turned hem suitable for fine fabrics.

nett edge of pattern

7mm (5/16in)

sew 3mm (1/8in) from fabric edge

Select a suitable size stitch in relation to fabric choice.

Roll the fabric against the first line of stitching to create a very narrow hem and sew a second line of stitching.

Roll the fabric against the second line of stitching and complete hem with a third line of stitching.

HEMMING STITCH

This is a handstitched hem finish that can be completed with a double-turned or overlocked finish. Working from right to left, bring the needle up through the hem edge. Directly opposite and fractionally above the hem, take a stitch, ensuring you catch only one or two threads of the fabric, then move the needle diagonally through the hem edge. Repeat for the length of the hem, spacing each stitch roughly 6–10mm (1/4–3/8in) apart; do not draw the thread tight as this will create a tension that will allow stitch work to show from the right side.

PATTERN DEVELOPMENT
Finishings, linings and facings

FACINGS

Facings are typically separate layers pattern-cut from the outer shell. They follow the same grainline as the outer and are usually cut in the self-fabric, though there are occasions where another material may be used – for both design and practical reasons. Facings have many purposes; they finish the edge of a garment as well as offering support to prevent distortion to profile edges. Because of the support they provide, facings are often interfaced, but it is important that the type of interfacing used is appropriate for both the fabric and the location. The facing should not be visible from the outside; therefore bulk (bulky fabric/interfacing) should be avoided.

Facings are often drafted 2mm ($\frac{1}{16}$in) smaller on the profile edge; this allows for the seam to be hidden on the inside. Here, when attaching the facing, the outer shell's edge is traditionally rolled inwards by 2mm ($\frac{1}{16}$in). The seam is then edge-stitched on the facing side; the stitch holds it in position and prevents it from showing.

The unattached edge of the facing must itself be finished in a suitable way for the type of garment, such as by overlocking or binding. To ensure that the facing stays in position, the facing should be caught along its length by 'invisibly' stitching (on the wrong side of the facing) onto the seam allowances that the panel intersects.

Facings can be used on their own or in conjunction with linings; the process to create the lining follows from those needed for the facing. This is covered in the next section.

COMMON AREAS FOR FACINGS

Common areas to face are the neckline, armhole (which can be combined with the neckline), hem, waist, jacket revers, vents/slits and garment openings. Facings are highly suitable for finishing shaped edges, such as a scalloped edge, where it would be near impossible to finish with any other method.

1. Fearne Cotton midi-panel dress.
(Photo credit: Very)

BODICE FACING

This method creates separate facings for the neck and armholes, and is suitable for tops and dresses.

On the back bodice, mark points at regular intervals, at around 4–5cm (1½–2in) in from both the neckline and armhole. Curve off the lines. To ensure a correct run, pattern pieces should be at right angles at the shoulder line, side seam and CF (1).

Repeat for front, making sure that the measurements at shoulder lines and side seam match (2).

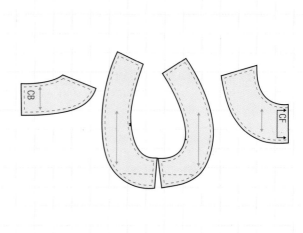

Trace off sections, adding seam allowances, pattern annotation, grainlines and so on.

To simplify the facing pattern and eliminate the bulk of an extra shoulder seam, the front and back sections can be combined.

PATTERN DEVELOPMENT
Finishings, linings and facings

ALL-IN-ONE FACING

An all-in-one facing is one where the outer shell is extended to include the facing. As this requires a folded (rather than seamed) edge, this can only be done for areas with straight profile edges, such as the CF on a shirt or top. This example creates an all-in-one facing that allows for a CF button fastening.

Decide on the size of the button. On the front bodice, draw a parallel line at a distance equal to the button diameter out from the CF; this will be the folded profile edge.

Draw a line from the bust line to the hem, parallel to the CF, about 6–7.5cm (2½–3in) in. Curve a line, as shown, from the bust to a point on the shoulder line around 5–6cm (2–2½in) down from the neck (2).

Mirror this facing section on the fold line (not the CF). Add seam allowances, notches, pattern annotation and grainlines (3).

JACKET FACING

This method creates facings to finish the profile edges, as well as back facing to stabilise the back neck, where the collar attaches.

On the jacket front, mark a line parallel to the CF, around 6–7.5cm (2½–3in) in, from the hem to a point level with the break point, at the start of the break line. From here, curve a smooth line up to a point on the shoulder line around 5–6cm (2–2½in) down from the neck. The line should make a right angle at the shoulder line.

Trace a copy, adding seam allowances and pattern annotation.

On the jacket back, mark a point on the shoulder line around 5–6cm (2–2½in) down from the neck. Mark a point at the same measurement down from the neckline at the CB, and then at regular intervals down from the neckline. Connect these points and curve off the line, ensuring a right angle at CB and shoulder line.

Mirror back pattern piece at CB. Add seam allowances, notches, pattern annotation and grainlines to all pieces.

For the sleeve facing, mark a section around 4–5cm (1½–2in) up from the hem.

Trace a copy, adding seam allowances and pattern annotation.

PATTERN DEVELOPMENT
Finishings, linings and facings

LININGS

Linings are an inner fabric shell, used on garments to hide the raw seam edges and internal structure (such as padding, interfacing or pocket bags). They also prevent wear and strain on the main garment body. Linings are drafted from the main garment pattern, and are mostly used in conjunction with facings (see previous section). An extra allowance is made to the lining pattern at areas such as the CB, armhole and hem so that the lining does not distort the outer shell when worn.

When choosing a lining fabric, it is important to choose a material that can move and give with the wearer; those that are smooth or silky, in addition, enable the garment to be put on more easily over other clothing. Fabrics such as viscose and acetate are often used as they both drape well and do not insulate body heat.

Some linings, such as on a traditional jacket, fully conceal the garment inner, whereas others may only be partially lined. A summer-weight jacket, for instance, could be lined solely on the fronts and the upper back, and with or without sleeve lining, so that interfacing and shoulder pads are hidden.

Linings do not always completely bag out the garment; a skirt or dress may be hemmed and left to hang separately (the lining hem overlapping the main garment hem). The lining is then held in position with chain-stitch loops.

CONSTRUCTING A LINED GARMENT

In a lined garment, the lining and outer are constructed separately, and then attached (bagged out) to each other by stitching around the garment profile edges.

1. Holly Willoughby crochet-collar tea dress.

(Photo credit: Very)

BASIC BODICE LINING WITH FRONT OPENING

Follow steps as for front and back bodice facings. Mark extra notches as shown. Draw desired width of hem facing, approx. 4–5cm (1½–2in).

Subtract facings from main body sections.

Pivot back shoulder dart into neckline; smooth curve at seam, leaving in dart amount as tolerance (ease). Pivot front shoulder dart into waistline.

A small bust pleat to add room and comfort can be put at this stage into the front armhole at a point below the front balance notch by pivoting part (2.5cm/1in) of the shoulder dart and the remainder into the waist.

At the bottom edge of the lining, add hem return of 2.5cm (1in). This creates a small pleat at the bottom of the lining. Redraw darts to the new edge, but keeping the original dart width. Add a box pleat at the back by adding 4cm (1½in) and tapering it down to the waist.

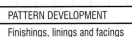

PATTERN DEVELOPMENT

Finishings, linings and facings

Combine facing pieces for front and back as shown; curve off angles where pieces join.

BACK NECK FACING
cut 1

CB

FRONT
FACING
cut 1 pair

CF

opening

BACK
ARMHOLE
FACING
cut 1 pair

FRONT
ARMHOLE
FACING
cut 1 pair

BACK
HEM FACING cut 1

Mirror facings at CB. Add seam allowances, notches and pattern annotation.

Add seam allowances and pattern annotation.

REDUCING BULK

When using thick fabrics, or widely spaced topstitching, it will be necessary to mitre the corners of the pocket prior to bagging out.

SKIRT LINING

Mark waistband facings on skirt.

Subtract facing sections from body of skirt to make lining.

Curve off top edge of lining, leaving in darts as tolerance (ease). If the remaining dart is more than 1.2cm (½in), half of the dart amount should be taken off the side seam, tapering to nothing at the hip (use the block to trace a new hip curve). Add an amount (2.5cm/1in) at the bottom edge to overlap the hem facing. Add the same amount again to create a hem return.

Mirror pattern pieces at CF and CB. Add seam allowances, notches and pattern annotation. Note how the front and back waist facings are created by closing the waist darts and smoothing the joins.

JACKET LINING

Follow steps as for front and back jacket facings.

Take away facing sections from main body.

Mark a point 4mm (³⁄₁₆in) up from front and back shoulder line at armhole; redraw new shoulder line, tapering to facing and new armhole, tapering to balance point. At underarm point on side seam, mark a point 1.5cm (⁵⁄₈in) up and 4mm (³⁄₁₆in) out; redraw new armhole tapering to balance, and new side seam tapering to waist.

Close dart at waist, opening to create pleat at armhole.

Create a pleat at the bottom of the sleeve lining by adding 2.5cm (1in) for the overlap of the sleeve hem facing and another 2.5cm (1in) for the hem lining return.

Remove hem return at back lining. On the front lining, curve a line up from the front edge at the hem return up to the side seam on the hemline. At CB add 2.5cm (1in), squaring down from the neck, and then tapering to the waist as shown. When sewn, this will create a pleat to add room for movement across the shoulders.

Add seam allowances and pattern annotation to finished pieces.

PATTERN DEVELOPMENT

Finishings, linings and facings

CHAPTER 13: POCKETS

Pockets can be functional, decorative or both. They can be applied or inserted into a garment, as in the case of a patch pocket, or form a structural element, such as the jeans-style pocket described below. Pockets can be cut to match or contrast with the grain of the garment.

Ensure that pockets are positioned and sized to be flattering on the final garment. You will notice that pockets are not always positioned on a true horizontal or vertical line, but are often angled to be more flattering. The chest welt pocket on a traditional man's suit is a good example of this: the pocket is angled slightly upwards, although it appears almost straight as it moulds around the body profile. An applied or inserted pocket, such as a patch pocket, can be added to a toile after the first fitting, once its position is ascertained in relation to the completed garment.

PATCH POCKETS

Patch pockets can come in any shape or size. The top of the pocket will require a turn-back (or hem) at the open edge of the pocket to provide stability and ensure the wrong side of the fabric does not show; in the case of a pocket with a shaped opening edge, a facing will be required.

UNLINED PATCH POCKET

Plan the pocket and turn-back, and mark the position of the pocket on the main pattern piece with drill holes.

Add turn-back onto patch pocket, add seam allowances and mark fold line with a notch.

Press seam allowances to wrong side and mitre corners. Sew turn-back hem.

Lightly press the turn-back.

reinforcement
stitches

RS

Sew to main garment, using backstitching or a more decorative stitch
to reinforce the pocket opening.

LINED PATCH POCKET

turn-back

fold line

Plan the pocket and turn-back, and
mark the position of the pocket on the
main pattern piece with drill holes.

POCKET LINING
cut 1 x lining

The lining is the pocket minus
turn-back. Add seam allowances.

turn-back

fold line

cut 1 x self

The pocket piece is the pocket
dimensions plus turn-back. Add seam
allowances and mark the fold line with
a notch.

lining WS

RS

Attach lining and pocket pieces
and press open seam allowances.

lining WS

Sew around the pocket, leaving an
opening to bag pieces out. Sew to
garment as for patch pocket.

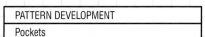

PATTERN DEVELOPMENT
Pockets

CURVED PATCH POCKETS

Plan pocket as for unlined patch pocket.

Fold and neaten the pocket facing. Loosen the upper tension on your machine and sew around the curve, leaving long threads to gauge the curve in the next step.

Pull bobbin thread tight, encouraging the SA to turn. Use a nett copy of the pocket as a pressing template and flatten the SA. Return tension to your usual setting and continue construction as for patch pocket.

PATCH POCKET WITH FLAP

Plan the pocket flap, extending the flap beyond the width of the patch pocket to ensure the flap covers the uppermost construction of the patch pocket.

Add 1cm (⅜in) seam allowance to pattern piece and label as pocket flap lining.

Make another copy of the pocket flap and add 3mm (⅛in) to the outer edge. Now add 1cm (⅜in) seam allowance to the pattern piece and label as pocket flap.

Bag out the pocket flap and complete with topstitching if necessary. Neaten the open edge of the pocket flap and secure to garment.

1. A patch pocket has been used in combination with a contrasting fabric to great effect in this dress.

(Photo credit: Internacionale)

POCKET IN SIDE SEAM

In its most simple form, a pocket bag is simply set in to the side seam and is cut in one piece with your garment. To reduce bulk or to minimise fabric costs, the pocket bag can be cut separately in lining or contrast fabric and the seam allowances offset to ensure the pocket seam does not show at the side seam. A strip of interfacing, or cotton tape, is positioned at the pocket opening to ensure that it does not stretch and sag during use.

SET-IN POCKET IN SEAM

Plan pocket and set in to front garment pattern piece.

Mirror pocket addition onto back pattern piece.

Sew side seam as one. For an open seam, mitre pocket pieces on front only or overlock front and back in one.

POCKET IN SEAM WITH SEPARATE POCKET BAG

Divide the pocket bag from the main pattern, setting the pocket seam back from the side seam to reduce unnecessary bulk.

With RS together, sew a pocket bag to front and back pattern pieces.

Sew side seam as one and mitre pocket pieces on front only, to press SA open or overlock front and back separately prior to joining side seam.

PATTERN DEVELOPMENT
Pockets

FRONT POCKETS

CURVED JEANS-STYLE FRONT POCKET

This pocket forms a structural element of the finished garment. Plan the pocket opening and the pocket bag, tracing off pieces as shown in the diagram. Note that the front side hip has a large seam allowance at its bottom edge to ensure that it is hidden by the pocket facing.

FRONT SIDE
HIP
cut 1 x self

POCKET
FUSING
cut 1 x fuse

HIP SECTION
cut 1 x lining

POCKET
FACING
cut 1 x lining

Overlock the edge of the front side hip and sew on top of hip section.

With right sides together, sew pocket facing to skirt.

under-stitch

Turn pocket facing to WS and under-stitch SA to pocket facing.

Fuse pocket opening on WS of skirt.

staystitch

neaten edges

Sew the hip section and pocket facing. Stitch the pocket opening.

Join side seams as usual, with right sides together.

TWO-PIECE WELT POCKET

fold line

WELT
cut 2 x self + fuse

POCKET BAG A
cut 1 x lining

POCKET BAG B
cut 1 x lining

Plan welt size. Draft welt pattern to 4 x welt width and add SA to outermost edges only. Mark fold with a notch. Plan the pocket bag depth. Draft pocket bag B to these measurements. Draft pocket bag A to same width plus welt pattern in length.

WS

Interface WS of fabric and mark welt opening with drill holes. Note that the innermost mark is 1cm (³⁄₈in) from outer edge.

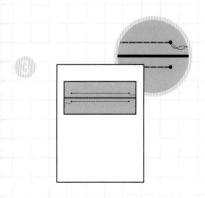

Lay welts onto main fabric with WS together and sew in line with drill holes.

cut along pocket opening on garment only

WS

Turn work over to WS and cut pocket opening on garment only, then mitre corners.

welts showing through

fold triangles of fabric to WS

WS

Fold along stitch line and post welts through pocket opening. Fold mitred triangles to WS.

PATTERN DEVELOPMENT
Pockets

Fold welts in half and lightly press. The welts can be tacked together at fold to stabilise during rest of construction.

Sew pocket bag A to uppermost welt along the stitch line created in stage 3.

Sew pocket bag B to lower welt along the stitch line created in stage 3.

Sew pocket bags together, ensuring that the mitred triangles are caught; neaten edges of pocket bag if required.

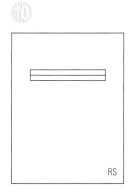

Finished pocket from right side.

WELT POCKET WITH FLAP

Draft flap pattern. Add 1 x welt width to top edge and 1cm (³⁄₈in) to sides and lower edge. Make another copy. Add 3mm (¹⁄₈in) to edge of one piece to allow for fabric loss while bagging out.

With RS together, sew pocket flap and pocket flap lining together, leaving one side open. Mitre corners and bag out. Topstitch if required.

The pocket flap is posted through pocket opening and the pocket bag is attached to welt and flap in one, as at stage 7 of welt construction.

Finished pocket from right side.

DRAFTING A FLAP ON THE FOLD

The flap can also be drafted on the fold and cut in 1 x self + interfacing. Cutting the flap on the fold reduces bulk and offers the opportunity to use a contrast fabric if desired.

1. Jacket with two-piece welt pocket.

(Photo credit: La Redoute)

PATTERN DEVELOPMENT
Pockets

ONE-PIECE WELT POCKET

Plan welt size. Draft welt piece at 2 x welt width and welt facing pattern to 1 x welt width plus 1.5cm (⅝in) to length. Add 1.5cm (⅝in) SA all around.

Plan pocket bag depth. Draft pocket bag to these measurements. Add 1.5cm (⅝in) SA and cut 2 x lining.

Interface WS of fabric and mark welt opening with drill holes. Note innermost drill hole is 1.5cm (⅝in) from outer edge.

Lay welts onto main fabric with WS together and sew in line with drill holes.

Turn work over to WS and cut pocket opening on garment only, then mitre corners.

Fold along stitch line and post welts through pocket opening. Fold mitred triangles to WS.

1. Selma tunic dress
with one-piece welt pocket.

(Photo credit: Want Her Dress)

Temporarily fold welt facing upwards and fold welt downwards, ready to attach the pocket bags.

With right sides together, sew one pocket bag to welt as shown in the diagram.

Fold welt in half and drop pocket bag into position, noting that the SA is facing towards the garment. Press SA open.

With RS together, sew the second pocket bag piece to welt facing.

Drop welt facing into position and press SA open. Sew pocket bags as for welt, if required, and neaten pocket bag as one.

Finished pocket from right side.

NOTE:

Note that the extra height added to the welt facing in stage 2 has enabled the SA to be offset, thus reducing unnecessary bulk.

PATTERN DEVELOPMENT

Pockets

4

THE DESIGNER MAKER

CHAPTER 14: GOING PRO   176
  • Design development   178
  • Technical considerations   182
  • Promoting your work   184

CHAPTER 14:
GOING PRO

Transforming a hobby into a business can be a big step; many people who work in this field have undertaken formal training or worked in an existing fashion company to learn the ins and outs of the business. However, many successful businesspeople can grow an enterprise from a passion or enthusiasm for their chosen field.

It is essential that you thoroughly research your market and ensure that you have a clear idea of your potential customer. Do you have a unique vision of your brand and the types of garments you wish to produce? Are you going to sell directly or via independent boutiques? Perhaps you also want to offer accessories such as scarves, belts or bags; these can offer an entry-level purchase, allowing your customer to buy into your brand at minimal cost.

You may need to start off performing every role, such as sourcing, design, construction and marketing. Spend your time wisely on the things that you do well, or where your time is put to best use. As your business grows, it is likely that you will need to outsource some elements of the collection. This will enable you to focus on other aspects, such as research (fabrics, trims, design development), merchandising and promoting the collection, as well as working with buyers. It can take time to build a successful brand; a good first step can be to work to commission or test the market with a small online store.

Feral Childe is a US-based womenswear line by bi-coastal design duo Moriah Carlson (Brooklyn, NY) and Alice Wu (Oakland, CA): www.feralchilde.com

Alexandra King is an independent bridal and womenswear label handmade in the UK: www.alexandra-king.com

ALEXANDRA KING

Gain as much experience as possible. Don't ever cut corners when it comes to the product. Don't over-indulge in equipment or fabrics, and believe in yourself, your value and your product. Be prepared for a lot of hard work, too.

1. Scroll tee and pleated skirt by Feral Childe.
(Photo credit: Feral Childe)

FERAL CHILDE

Start locally! Know your customer. Learn how to sell. Keep that day job for as long as you can and work for other fashion companies, both big and small. If you work for a small company you'll see what it's going to be like running your own company.

DESIGN DEVELOPMENT

Collections are usually divided into seasons: spring/summer and autumn/winter, with other smaller releases such as a resort or pre-collection bridging the main collections. Large main collections can be further divided into launches, with individual themes and colour palettes, that will enter the market at different stages. This cycle may or may not be appropriate to your business model.

In the industry, the design cycle often begins with fabric and trim sourcing. Fabrics, trims and fastenings can be sourced in many ways. To get the best deal, especially if bigger quantities are wanted, go straight to the supplier or wholesaler rather than buying through a retailer. Note, however, that most of these companies have a minimum order, which may be prohibitive. It is important that you select materials and trims that reflect not only your spending power but also have working properties that are appropriate to the intended garments contained within your range.

When beginning a new collection, gather together concepts and design details that excite and inspire you as a designer. Sources of inspiration can come from everywhere and anywhere. It is important to keep your mind open; quite often ideas come from completely diverse places to create exciting and new contrasts.

FERAL CHILDE

We often begin with very abstract ideas – loosely connected themes not directly related to fashion or clothing at all.

SKETCHBOOKS AND MOOD BOARDS

Sketchbooks are not only the best place to keep ideas and store photographs and clippings, they're also perfect for recording technical notes and sketches to ensure you fully develop design ideas. Do not be put off if you feel you do not draw particularly well or are rusty: practice will make it easier for you to convey your ideas in this format, and observations from life or photography will improve your 3D 'vocabulary'. Experiment with different media such as collage, watercolours or marker pens to communicate your ideas. A fashion croquis, or figure, can be invaluable for getting your initial ideas down quickly.

1. A sketchbook page with ideas for accessories.

(Photo credit: Feral Childe)

FERAL CHILDE

We try to use the most sustainable materials we can find. This means natural fibres from silks to organic cotton, linen, Tencel and hemp blends. Another option is to use vintage deadstock or surplus fabrics left over from other manufacturers. Sometimes we'll use these fabrics as is, but we have also given them new life by overdyeing or overprinting.

Mood boards can be a more focused version of the sketchbook and are a great way of communicating the feel of a collection. Find a format that works best for you, whether this is on presentation boards, large polystyrene pinboards, a CAD presentation or even a video mood board.

**The Autumnal
Travelling Tinker**
Autumn/Winter 2012

FERAL CHILDE

About 70 per cent of the collection is built from past patterns because we always offer a certain number of variations on past bestsellers/ staples. We update and improve the fit of these and reinterpret them in different fabrics, which requires us to adapt the pattern.

BUILDING A COLLECTION

The key to a successful, cohesive collection is good design development. It is important to remember that the design process does not end with an illustration of your proposed design but also includes the thorough investigation of each garment in terms of silhouette, proportion and detailing. Before settling on your final idea, sketch it out multiple times, playing with design details such as pocket placement, topstitching or finishing methods. Constantly ask yourself questions. How does one get into the garment? Is that the best length for the skirt or bodice? Would this particular garment look better with a large full sleeve or one that is closer-fitting? Each design decision has repercussions on the pattern drafting and construction processes; thorough attention to design development ensures that you are planning ahead and have a good working drawing of a garment that is actually achievable.

Your business model may entail the creation of 'one off' garments or the cyclical production of a collection of garments. When creating multiple items within one release, range planning becomes key. It is important that you begin to think in terms of a capsule collection, ensuring that pieces interact as a whole. Repeating design features across different garments within your range can help to build a cohesive look. The fashion industry appears to be focused on constant reinvention and pressure to keep reinventing the wheel, but do not be distracted by this. Styles from previous seasons can be updated with new design details and used as a basis for new garments within your next collection.

PRICING YOUR PRODUCT

A small fashion producer will find it very difficult to compete with prices in the mass market; you need to offer your clients something different and of a sufficiently good quality to justify the prices you will need to set as an independent designer.

The design process not only includes the themes and ideas behind your collection but also entails keeping tight control over the total cost of your final product. Be aware that you will need to keep an eye on the running costs of your business, including materials, manufacturing costs, machinery and utilities, before you even start to turn a profit and pay yourself for your services. You may find you need to make compromises as you go along, and it is important you do not overspend, thus pricing yourself out of the market.

TECHNICAL CONSIDERATIONS

To be able to outsource elements of a collection, such as print and embroidery, or the pattern cutting and construction of the garment as a whole, the most vital thing is good communication. For the factories or outsourced freelancers who are involved in garment drafting and production, a clear technical drawing and specification sheet for each garment is imperative. The sewing contractor must be able to understand each detail so a successful interpretation of the garment can be made.

TECHNICAL DRAWING

Technical drawings are a precise and proportional rendering of your design; illustrative devices such as the stylistic lengthening of the figure, which often occurs in a fashion sketch, are not used. This type of drawing is often referred to as a 'flat', which indicates that the garment is drawn as it appears laid flat. It is essential that both front and back views are included; some designs may also warrant a side view. The flat should also include any details such as topstitching, button placement and seam construction, alongside some basic working measurements such as neckline drops, skirt/bodice lengths and opening positions. A well-annotated technical drawing serves as a reference throughout the drafting and manufacturing process.

SPECIFICATION SHEETS

A specification sheet also contains a technical drawing and is a standardised guide for quality control both in-house and throughout the manufacturing chain. It exhibits more detailed finishing details and contains a column for precise measurements of both pattern and garment. The final column shows the 'tolerance', or acceptable margin of difference, between the two.

ALEXANDRA KING

I made lots of mistakes when starting out; mainly this was due to undervaluing myself, as many creatives do. It can be terrifying trying to sell your personal work, but when you have your product perfected it's easy to stand by it and believe in yourself.

A specification sheet will include the following information, as relevant to the individual design:

- Lengths of important parts of the garment, such as openings, cuff/waistband widths, collar size, hem length, and details such as pockets and flaps.

- Type and code of fastening, with exact details of colour and finish.

- Codes and colour of fabric, and where they are used.

- Topstitching, thread colour, size of stitch and distance from seam (e.g., ¼ stitch).

- Codes and colour of trimmings, such as drawstrings, ribbon or eyelets.

- Any embroidery or print placements.

- Costing and consumption information.

The example specification sheet shown here contains the minimum information that should be logged for each garment. In industry this document may be referred to as a Specification or Technical Pack and will also include detail such as labelling and grading information.

SEASON/DATE:
Style Ref:
Description:

FABRIC/TRIM:
Self/Main:
Contrast:
Lining:
COLOUR:

SKETCH AND MEASUREMENT POSITIONS:

MEASUREMENT POSITIONS	PATTERN	GARMENT	TOLERANCE
a front length: SNP to hem – in a waisted style ensure you specify to waist seam or hem			
b back length: CB to hem, CB to waist, etc.			
c neckline straight: SNP to SNP			
d front neckline drop			
e back neckline drop			
f shoulder			
g across back ½ – usually measured 4³/₄in (12cm) down from CB neckline but ensure you specify			
h arm hole ½ – if garment has a sleeve this can be measured straight, no sleeve measure along curve			
i across bust ½ – usually measured 1in (2.5cm) down from underarm seam but ensure this is specified			
j waist ½ – specify distance from underarm			
k hem ½ straight – a flared hem should be laid flat to record this measurement			
l hem dip – specify CF or CB			
m side seam – in a waisted style, ensure you specify to/from waist seam, etc.			
n overarm sleeve length			
o underarm sleeve length			
p bicep ½ – usually 1in (2.5cm) from underarm seam but ensure you specify			
q elbow ½ – fold sleeve so hem touches underarm seam and measure the sleeve across the fold			
r cuff ½			
s cuff width			
t waist seam to pocket			
u pocket position: specify position from nearest seams			
v pocket depth			
w pocket width			

PROMOTING YOUR WORK

Branding, marketing and merchandising are central when building
a collection. They encompass everything including the logo, packaging
and hangtags, to convey a cohesive look and message to the consumer.
Marketing is the method by which you present the collection: advertising,
an online presence such as a website or a blog, catwalk presentations or trunk
shows. Lookbooks are a selling and promotional tool that can be as creative
as you like and can sell the story of your collection. Your mood board and/or
selected pages from your sketchbook can be collated to form the backbone
of this type of presentation. Line sheets are slightly more staid and contain
technical drawings, fabric, colour and pricing information; it is these, as well
as a sample garment, that potential buyers from retail outlets will be most
interested in.

Social media and the internet enable you to interact directly with potential
customers and can help to create a buzz around your collection and product.
This method is increasingly harnessed by big brands and smaller independent
designers alike. A blog or picture-hosting website can be an excellent way to
begin building your brand identity without the expense of website design and
hosting. It is best to post regularly rather than sporadically, as this will keep
your readers' interest up. Consider posting sneak peeks of your workspace or
imagery and music or design that inspires you. Tagging uploaded content with
appropriate words to describe content as well as your name will start to move
you up the search-engine listings. The use of analytic tools can allow you to
gain a good understanding of your market and the search terms by which
traffic is being directed to your site.

ALEXANDRA KING

I present the collections online in lots of detail along with a build-up
to the launch with all of our development images and inspirations.

1. Sewn-in garment labels.

(Photo credit: Feral Childe)

FERAL CHILDE

We photograph the collections
and harness social media to
continue our outreach to stores
and customers.

E-TAILING

Electronic retailing, or e-tailing, is the term coined to describe the buying and
selling of retail goods via the internet. This type of retailing can be particularly
suitable as a first step for your fashion entrepreneurship, benefiting from zero
or minimal set-up costs compared to those of a physical retail space. Many
e-commerce sites have formed a partnership with PayPal, enabling the secure
sale of goods to anyone with an email address without the need for a credit card.

You may choose to set up your own stand-alone website to retail your goods,
but there is also a wide variety of e-commerce marketplaces such as Etsy,
which allow for personal storefronts among peer retailers. A potential e-tail
customer may hold a natural apprehension regarding sizing, which can be
overcome by providing some of the collated information from a specification
sheet for comparison against personal measurements.

GLOSSARY

bagging out: to stitch two sections together, sewing around profile edges with right sides together. With one part left open, the section is then turned through, or 'bagged out', enclosing all seams. Sections that are typically bagged out are collars and linings.

bias: a grain with natural stretch that runs diagonally at 45 degrees to the selvedge.

balance: the proper 'hang' or 'fall' of a garment.

balance points: similar to notches, but used on a nett pattern for measuring pieces together and checking balance (e.g., sleeve pitch).

bishop sleeve: a sleeve that is fitted at the top and gathered into the cuff, using flare to make the extra fullness at the cuff.

block: a basic pattern that can be used as a starting point for drafting many styles of garment. Sometimes referred to as a 'sloper'.

break line: the line at which the rever naturally folds back.

break point: the point at which the rever starts to fold back to form the lapel.

cap sleeve: a very short sleeve. Can be drafted by slightly extending the shoulder line, so that it 'caps' the shoulder, or can be set-in.

close a dart: to remove a dart so that it can be transferred, or 'opened' in another position.

collar point: the pointed end of the collar where the lead edge and leaf edge meet.

construction lines: lines on the pattern giving specific information, e.g., dart position.

cut 1 pair: cut one plus a mirrored opposite.

cut 2: cut two identical pieces.

cut to fold/cut on fold: creates a mirrored piece from a half-section. This method is not used in mass industry. Fold a section of fabric and place fold line on pattern to fold.

darts: a form of suppression found, for example, around the bust, waist and hips. These are stitched sections, usually triangular or diamond-shaped, that take in areas of excess fabric as shaping.

dolman: a set-in sleeve that has a dropped armhole, but plenty of 'lift' due to extra fabric being added at the underarm.

drafting: the creation of a basic block.

drape: the amount of extra fabric at the underarm, which allows the sleeve to be lifted comfortably. Common in dolman and kimono sleeves.

edge-stitching: topstitching sewn closely (i.e., 3mm/⅛in/) to the edge of the seam, or garment profile.

fall: the part of the collar that 'falls' over, between the roll line and style line.

flat collar: a collar that sits flat around the shoulders.

fullness: extra fabric added to a pattern piece for shaping that can be used as flare, gather or tolerance.

graded nest: a visual 'stack' containing each size grade of a pattern piece, from smallest to largest.

grading: the practice of sizing a pattern piece up or down using set incremental grade rules, or measurements.

grain: the thread direction of the fabric. Although it can refer to either warp or weft, the term 'grain' is commonly used in connection with the warp.

grainline: a straight line on the pattern piece that denotes the direction in which the pattern should lay, parallel to the warp.

increment: the specific amount in which size groups differ; to incrementally enlarge or decrease the pattern size.

interfacing: a textile used to stabilise another fabric. These can be either fusible or sewn-in, and are available in numerous weights and qualities.

lapel: the part of a rever that folds back over the break line and lays flat on the front.

lead edge: the front edge of a collar, e.g., the edges on a shirt collar between which the tie would sit.

leaf edge/style line: the outer edge of the collar.

leg-of-mutton: a very full sleeve, gathered into the armhole, and gathered in at the elbow. The sleeve is then closely fitted from the elbow to the wrist. Common in Victorian times.

lift: the amount a sleeve can be moved comfortably when the arm is raised, without distorting the garment.

lining: an inner shell of the garment, made of a lighter-weight fabric, that encloses all the internal seams.

mirrored piece: a symmetrical pattern piece, which, flipped on a mirror line, creates the complete garment section.

mitre: to cut away bulk from seam allowances at corners diagonally, so that they can be turned through fully, ensuring a sharp profile edge.

nett: a piece or section of pattern without seam allowance.

nett pattern: a pattern without seam allowance.

notches: small snips made in the seam allowance to mark where two garment pieces are to be matched and sewn together.

profile: the outer edge of a garment or garment section.

quarter-stitch: topstitching 6mm (¼in) in from the profile edge. Seen on shirt collars and cuffs.

raglan: a sleeve that has the shoulder sections of the back and front bodice all in one, so that the sleeve extends up to the neck.

rever: a collar that is partially grown on to the front, and forms a permanent fold-back, as on a man's tailored jacket.

roll: a small amount of extra fabric given to allow a seam to be 'rolled' so that the seam edge is hidden. Found, for example, on collars and revers.

run: the edge created when two pattern pieces join, such as the underarm, or the crotch. This line should 'run' smoothly, rather than bump.

seam allowance (SA): an extra amount (for example 1.5cm/½in) added around the pattern to allow for garment pieces to be seamed together.

self/main: the main fabric of the garment.

selvedge: the self-finished edges of the fabric. Derived from 'self-edge'.

set-in sleeve: a sleeve that is sewn in to a completely made-up armhole, i.e. the shoulder and side seams are sewn before the sleeve is sewn in.

sink-stitch: to stitch 'invisibly' into, or through, one seam, to attach another garment part underneath, such as a waistband facing. Also known as stab-stitching.

size chart: a standardised guide of body measurements for each size grade.

sleevehead: the (usually curved) section at the top of a sleeve, which is sewn into the armhole.

sleeve pitch: the correct 'hang' of the sleeve. Balance points, and accurate cutting, will control this.

square-off: to mark a line at a right angles (90 degrees) to another.

stand: the part of the collar that stands up around the neck. Usually separate, e.g., on shirt collars. It can also be concealed.

suppression: shaping such as darts, tucks or gathers, which take in excess fabric.

toile: a test version of a garment, normally made in cotton fabric.

tolerance: an amount of fullness given to a garment to achieve a more comfortable fit; also known as 'ease'. With seams that have been 'eased in', the excess should be invisible and not gathered.

topstitch: a line of stitching that is seen on the right side of the fabric, sewn usually in a larger stitch length with topstitching thread. Topstitching can be both functional (adding strength to seams) and decorative.

twin-needle stitching: two, typically parallel, rows of stitching. Found, for example, on jeans pockets.

warp: the lengthwise yarns of the fabric, which run parallel to the edge.

weft: yarns that run across the fabric, at right angles to the edge.

wrap: the extra fabric added onto a collar and centre front to enable the fronts to overlap and fasten up.

RESOURCES

USEFUL SOFTWARE

Fittingly Sew
PC-compatible CAD program for designing and drafting sewing patterns.

Garment Designer 2.5
PC- and Mac-compatible CAD program for designing and drafting sewing patterns.

USEFUL WEBSITES

Fashion Incubator
www.fashion-incubator.com
Networking and advice from industry professionals.

Flickr
www.flickr.com
Online photo-sharing and management application.

Grade House
www.gradehouse.co.uk
Grading and costing services.

Ponoko
www.ponoko.com
3D printing and laser-cutting 'Personal Factory' facilitating the making and selling of custom products: think laser-cut accessories such as jewellery or buttons.

Spoonflower
www.spoonflower.com
Design and retail custom-printed fabric on demand with no minimum order.

Style.com
Style.com
Fashion news and trend reporting with extensive coverage of fashion shows.

RETAIL WEBSITES

ASOS
www.asos.com
Offers storefronts for vintage and fashion e-tailers.

Etsy
www.etsy.com
Handmade and vintage marketplace offering personal storefronts.

FashionStake
www.fashionstake.com
Online fashion boutique for professional independent designers.

Not Just a Label
notjustalabel.com
Showcase and retail platform for contemporary fashion.

FURTHER READING

Bray, Natalie, ***Dress Pattern Designing***
(John Wiley & Sons), 2003

Bray, Natalie, ***More Pattern Designing***
(John Wiley & Sons), 2003

Fasanella, Kathleen, ***The Entrepreneur's Guide to Sewn Product Manufacturing***
(Apparel Technical Services), 1998

Hagger, Ann, ***Pattern Cutting for Lingerie, Beachwear and Leisurewear***
(John Wiley & Sons), 2004

Nakamichi, Tomoko, ***Pattern Magic 1 & 2***
(Laurence King Publishing), 2010 & 2011

INDEX

A-line skirts 74
abdomen 93
accessories 176
adding seam allowances 58
adding volume 107
all-in-one button stands 136–37
all-in-one cap sleeves 122
all-in-one facings 156
analytic tools 184
annotation 6–7
armholes 83–84
arms 86–88
arrangement of order 43
assembling 43
asymmetric darts 64

back 91–92
back shoulder to armhole dart 63
back shoulder to neckline dart 63
bagged-out sections 135
basic blocks 50–53
bias shapes 110
bishop sleeves 108
blocks 50–53
bodice facing 155
bodice lining 159–60
bodices 79–80, 107, 110
boning 32
bound plackets 142
bound seams 24
box pleats 115
brands 176, 184
broad shoulders 82
bust 89–90
button stands 136–39
buttonholes 139
buttons 147

cap sleeves 122
cape block 119
capes 119–21
Carlson, Moriah 176
centre-back openings 130
checking grain 36
circle skirts 72–73
closing 43
collars 124–29
collections 181
commissions 176
concealed zips 150
contour darts 27
corner seams 20
cowl bodices 110
crown height 85

cuffs 134–35
culotte block 55
culottes 54–55
curved darts 28, 64
curved jeans-style front pockets 168–69
curved patch pockets 166
curved seams 21
cutting bias shapes 110
cutting collars 124
cutting fabrics 34, 41

dart manipulation 60–64
dart tucks 28
darts 26–29, 57, 59–64, 117
decorative tolerance 109
decorative elbow darts 117
decorative yokes 69
design development 178–81
directional sewing 18
double-turn hems 153
drape 98–103, 110–11
dress block 50, 51, 70

e-tailing 185
ease 84, 87, 109
easy-fit body 75
easy-fit sleeves 76
edge-stitched seams 19
elbows 88, 117
empire line 70
erect back 91
essential items 10–12
Eton collars 126
Etsy 185, 189

fabrics 30–45
facings 154–57
fastenings 146–51
Feral Childe 176–79, 181, 185
fine fabrics 40
finishing 43
finishing seams 18
fitting abdomen 93
fitting back 91–92
fitting hips 93
fitting shoulders 81
fitting sleeves 84–88
flapped welt pockets 171
flat collars 125
flat method, rub-off drafting 94–97
flat-felled seams 22
fluted hems 120
French darts 62
French seams 22

front openings 159–60
front pockets 168–73
full-fluted hems 120
fusible interfacings 31

gaping armholes 84
garment-construction equipment 12
gathering 112–13
glossary 186–88
grain 34–36
grainless fabrics 35
grain placement 114

hemming stitch 153
hems 120–21, 152–53
high bust 89
high rounded back 91
hips 93
hooks and eyes 147

identifying grain 35
interfacings 30–31
inverted box pleats 115
invisible zips 146, 151
invisible separating zips 146

jacket facings 157
jacket linings 162–63
jackets 45, 98–103
jeans-style front pockets 168–69

King, Alexandra 176, 182, 184

large abdomen 93
large armholes 83
large arms 86
large bust 90
large upper arms 88
layout 34, 40
leg-of-mutton sleeves 109
length adjustment 78
lightweight invisible zips 146
line sheets 184
lined jackets 45
lined patch pockets 165
linings 158–63
linking 43
lookbooks 184
low bust 89
low necklines 59, 124
low-rise waistbands 133
lowering dart apex 59
lowering necklines 124

machine feet 14
machine-rolled hems 153
Mandarin collars 127
marketing 184
marking buttonholes 139
marking fabrics 6, 34, 41
marking tools 13
marking zips 148
matching seams 17
matching thread 17
measurements 48–49, 56, 183, 185
merchandising 176, 184
mid-shoulder drape 111
mirroring pleats 115
mitreing corners 20, 160
mood boards 178–79, 184
moving darts 60

narrow back 92
narrow shoulders 82
narrow waistbands 130
necklines 59, 124
notches 24

one-piece placket bands 144–45
one-piece welt pockets 172–73
online stores 176, 185
openings 130, 136–45, 159–60
order of make 42–45
outsourcing 176

panelled skirts 71
patch pockets 164–66
patch pockets with flaps 166
pattern design essentials 56–59
patterned fabrics 38
PayPal 185
Peter Pan collars 125
pile direction 39
piped seams 25
plackets 140–45
plain seams 19
plain zips 146
pleats 114–15
pockets 164–73
posture 48
preparing fabrics 37–38
preparing seams 16
pressing darts 29
pressing tools 13
pricing 181
princess line 67
printed fabric 38
professional design 176–85
profit 181
promotion 176, 184–85
prototypes 77

raglan sleeves 118
reinforced darts 29
resources 189
retail websites 189
rever collars 129
right sides of fabric 38
rounded back 91
rub-off drafting 94–103
rub-off jackets 98–103
rub-off skirt 95–97
ruffles 112
run of pattern 56
running costs 181

seams 16–25, 58, 166
search-engine listings 184
semicircle skirts 73
semi-concealed zips 149
semi-fitted sleeves 117
separate button stands 138–39
separate pocket bags 167
separating zips 146
set-in pockets 167
sewing gathers 113
sewing machines 14–15
shaped cuffs 134
shaped darts 28
shaped waistbands 131–32
shirring 112
shirt collars 128–29
shirt cuffs 134
shirt sleeve plackets 140–42
shirt yokes 68
shirts 45, 68, 128–29, 134, 140–42
shoulder darts 63, 66
shoulder pads 32–33
shoulder and waist darts 63
shoulder point darts 63
shoulder to armhole darts 61
shoulder to centre front darts 62
shoulder to neckline darts 61
shoulders 81–82
side-seam openings 130
side-seam pockets 166
sides of fabric 38
sketchbooks 178
skirt block 52, 54, 55, 71
skirt lining 161
skirts 45, 71–72, 74, 79–80, 95–97
sleeve block 50
sleeve guards 140–42
sleeve insertion 44
sleeveless styles 83
sleeves 78, 80, 84–88, 108–9, 116–23, 140–45
sloping shoulders 81

small bust 90
smocking 112
snaps 147
software 189
specification sheets 182–83
split darts 63
square shoulders 81
standard dart positions 60
staystitching 18
straight waistbands 130
straightening grain 36
style lines 65
symmetry 40

tacking 17
taking measurements 48–49
taping seams 18
technical drawing 182
templates 50
thick elbows 88
thin arms 87
three waist darts 63
tight armholes 83
toiles 50, 77, 94
tolerance 84, 87, 109
trimming darts 27
trimming seams 18
trousers 45
truing-up darts 57
tubular sleeve insertion 44
turn-and-overlock hems 152
two-piece sleeves 122–23
two-piece welt pockets 169–70

underarm darts 61
understitching 20
upper arms 88

Vienna line 65–66
visible zips 148
volume 106–7

waistbands 130–33
websites 184–85, 189
wedge darts 27
welt pockets 169–73
welt seams 23
wide back 92
wide waistbands 130
width adjustments 80
wrong sides of fabric 38
Wu, Alice 176

yokes 68–69

zips 146

THE DESIGNER MAKER
Index

ACKNOWLEDGEMENTS

Jo and Andrew would like to extend huge appreciation to RotoVision, and to all those who have contributed to the book – in particular: Lindy Dunlop, Isheeta Mustafi, Emily Portnoi, Nicola Hodgson and Rebecca Stephenson. A big thank you is also owed to our colleagues at Bath Spa University and City of Bath College, and to the designers Alexandra King and Feral Childe for their contributions.

Jo would like to give a big shout out to Mr Freeman, Mrs Skirty, Miss Leake and, of course, Mr Richards.

Andrew would also like to thank Lucinda, Jacky and Jo.